children's spaces
from zero to ten

children's spaces
from zero to ten

Judith Wilson

photography by Debi Treloar

RYLAND
PETERS
& SMALL
LONDON NEW YORK

0977442666

Senior designer **Louise Leffler**
Senior editor **Annabel Morgan**
Location manager **Kate Brunt**
Production director **Meryl Silbert**
Art director **Gabriella Le Grazie**
Publishing director **Alison Starling**

Stylist **Judith Wilson**

First published in the United Kingdom in 2001
by Ryland Peters & Small
20–21 Jockey's Fields
London WC1R 4BW

10 9 8

ISBN 1 84172 120 4

A CIP record for this book is available from the British Library.

www.rylandpeters.com

contents

Kids get everywhere, whatever space they're given. Newly arrived, the tiniest baby has enough equipment to rival a squaddie. And, from the minute a child becomes mobile, not a square centimetre of your precious home will be sacred. Children are noisy, exuberant and have stuff by the crate load. They may drive the style queens among us to the edge, yet without them home would be too pristine a place.

This book won't maintain your hard-won, carefully designed space at the expense of your kids' physical and creative freedom. It won't

introduction

teach you to stencil a teddy-bear border, either. Instead, there is plenty of inspiration here from real families, with real kids, who amply prove that children and great design can co-exist happily, without either party having to compromise on style. Armed with practical surfaces and effective storage systems, parents can reclaim communal living areas within a matter of seconds at bedtime and enjoy being grown-ups again. And your kids will appreciate a vibrant, stimulating environment that is practical and relaxed too.

Whether you're adapting a sophisticated, child-free zone for the arrival of a new baby, or starting from scratch because your small children have just outgrown a current home, some serious thinking is required. Plan all the practical aspects first, and the design and decoration will be a breeze. Your kids' needs may seem obvious, but their demands change with alarming speed. This is even more crucial with a new baby. Impossible as it may seem, that chubby infant kicking on a rug will all too soon demand a space and life of its own.

If your style is streamlined and modern, celebrate. A contemporary interior is perfect for kids: planes of colour and sleek surfaces make a marvellous backdrop for toys, paintings and accessories. The rules are simple: things must be practical as well as looking good, and children must be taught to respect what the whole family shares. Don't think that little ones are naturally inclined to dayglo colours and cute motifs. Credit them with good taste, involve your kids in planning their spaces and give everyone (including yourself) licence for fun and a free rein.

A baby's first room needs tranquillity and comfort, for infant and parents alike. Keep things simple with clear colours, quick-access storage and a great view from the cot. Sensory touches add magic; perhaps a wind chime or twinkling fairy lights.

rooms for babies

1

A baby needs little in the early days, though department stores might try to persuade you otherwise. Many infants don't even move into their own room until three months or beyond, perfectly content to swing in a cradle at their parents' bedside. Nevertheless, a new arrival does need its own bedroom, for nappy changing, storing clothes and to house a nascent collection of toys. A small room is fine. It is cosy, and most toddlers would rather play in the family space downstairs than in a bedroom.

The main nursery basic is a cot. Simple styles are both practical and chic. More enticing options than traditional varnished pine are beech or cherrywood cots (though they will cost more), white-painted wood, colourful melamine or decorative ironwork. An antique or retro-style cot can look beautiful in a pared-down room but, for peace of mind, check that its dimensions meet British Standards guides and always buy a new mattress. A cot bed, with slatted sides that are removed as the baby grows up, is a sensible, cost-effective option. Pick the plainest style you can find.

Frilly, character-emblazoned bumpers and valances will spoil the look of a simple, contemporary nursery. A padded bumper is a good idea because it protects restless little heads, but choose one in plain colours and with quilting, not frills. Cotton sheets and blankets and a comforting quilt are the other basics. When your baby is a year old, you can add a baby pillow and cot duvet. Nursery manufacturers have become increasingly inventive in recent years, so blankets and sheets now come in every shade from pretty pastels to vibrant hues. It's fun to pick and choose between different co-ordinated ranges, or add a retro piece or two.

THIS PAGE AND OPPOSITE: **In a baby girl's nursery, a whitewashed antique cot with a cut-out heart motif sets the tone for a simple yet pretty room. Pastel-painted peg rails hung with tiny dresses brighten white walls. Painted pieces of board with old-fashioned wooden pegs attached allow** **for an ever-changing display of nostalgic pictures, family snaps and paintings – there's always something stimulating for baby to contemplate. Open shelves (above) are a user-friendly and decorative way to stack baby clothes, but allocate one alcove to each clothes type to avoid muddles.**

Team a pink gingham sheet with a tangerine blanket, or add a home-made Noddy pillowcase to perk up plain white linens. A large single motif on a blanket looks smarter than a tiny repeated design.

The nappy changing area should be efficient and fuss-free. Resist the temptation to buy a specialist unit; it will soon be redundant. A chest of drawers at the correct height, with a plastic padded mat on top, can double up as a changing area. Store all the essential kit – nappies, wipes and creams – in the drawers immediately below, hidden away from inquisitive toddler siblings. Alternatively, place them on a chunky MDF shelf above the chest but within arm's reach. If you have enough space, consider designing a custom-made unit. You will need alcoves for clothes, cotton wool, nappies and so on, with a discreet pull-out or pull-down changing surface. If the changing mat is going to be on permanent view, pick one of the trendier designs. Funky fake grass or cloud images have a distinct edge over teddy bears. Hang a mobile above the mat: kids' mail-order catalogues often feature abstract ones, like trendy clips from which you can hang postcards or photographs.

A low, comfortable armchair is a must for feeding. Get a loose cover made in a sturdy, washable fabric – bright denim, robust linen or towelling. If there's enough floor space, beanbags in jelly-bean colours or wipe-clean vinyl cubes are great for babies learning to sit up or crawl.

Keep the room looking modern with fuss-free window treatments. If you'd prefer little ones not to wake with the dawn chorus, use blackout lining. A roller blind, Roman blind or wooden shutters are simple and neat; or, if you'd rather have curtains, bright or strong pastel plains, checks or children's motif fabrics make the best choices. If you choose the latter, go for classic children's characters; they look more stylish than today's garish and over-publicized images. Or look to the more exclusive fabric houses, which often carry whimsical, abstract kids' designs at reasonable prices.

Plain painted walls and an easy-care floor create the most restful environment for a baby. Choose colours that you like for the early years – babies don't form their tastes this young. Whitewashed walls and a neutral floor create the perfect background for colourful accessories. But if you (and baby) need stimulation, paint one wall in a bold shade like cherry red or swimming-pool turquoise. If you prefer soothing pastels, stronger tones like lavender or duck-egg blue make the best background for primary-coloured toys. Try painting abstract shapes: stripes or giant dots look good. Don't forget the ceiling – babies spend hours on their backs.

THIS PAGE AND OPPOSITE:
This double divan with surround on a tubular frame is ideal for a toddler who has outgrown a cot but is not yet ready for a bed. In this room, blocks of strong colour create a bold contemporary mood – the egg-yolk yellow walls, purple drawer unit, scarlet duvet and lime chair are stimulating and jolly. The practical clothes storage includes a rack for dresses and shoes (opposite below), while a painted chest of drawers doubles up as a baby changing unit.

THIS PAGE AND OPPOSITE: With its sloping ceilings, an attic room makes for a bright, cosy nursery. Take advantage of a skylight view by placing the cot directly beneath the window, but don't forget a blackout blind or shutters to cut out glare. Toddler Scarlet's room proves that pink and white, that classic little girl's colour combination, can be fresh and pretty instead of fussy and twee. White walls, a white cot and neutral carpeting provide the basic backdrop, while clear, cool pink accessories provide decorative accents.

Crouch down by the cot and experience your baby's-eye view, then give him or her intriguing moving stimuli. Can your baby see through the window and spy trees, or view clouds through a skylight? If not, reposition the cot. String the ceiling with colourful Chinese lanterns, party bunting or paper mobiles. You don't have to cover the walls with pictures, but you and the baby need something to look at. Initiate a personal collection now: a framed baby handprint or informal black-and-white baby portraits are more arresting images than most conventional children's art.

Use imaginative lighting to add a creative dimension. If there's an overhead light, fit it with a dimmer switch, essential for checking on the baby at night. Plunder both adult and children's lighting departments for unusual options. As well as 'magic lantern' children's lamps, which splash the walls with gentle colour and movement, consider a lava lamp, strings of flower fairy lights, illuminated globes or punched-metal lampshades that cast pretty patterns. Buy a packet of light-up stars for walls and ceiling, to glow long after lights-out.

THIS PAGE AND OPPOSITE: The simple, neutral look won't suit every parent or every baby. One way to customize a tiny boxroom – often the only space available for a new baby – is to douse it in colour. In baby Archie's bedroom, the walls are transformed with zany stripes, while the cot was chosen for its innovative silhouette and zesty lime colour. For similar stripes, paint walls in a strong base colour – hot pink was used here – then use masking tape to mark out stripes of varying widths. For simpler splashes of colour, paint blank artists' canvases in bold shades and hang them around the room.

LEFT: **Give plenty of thought to nursery storage, then get a carpenter to build it to your specifications. This cupboard has a pull-out changing surface and tailor-made box to hold nappy wipes, plus shelves for nappies. It also acts as a divider between the baby's sleeping space and play area.**

BELOW, LEFT TO RIGHT: **Not all babies have the luxury of their own room. Sliding doors partition off this little girl's cot from an open-plan loft (left). A cot in a corner of the parents' bedroom can be individualized in small decorative ways, with baby photos (centre) or lengths of colourful bunting (right).**

You'll probably need more space for baby clothes than you expect. Little vests and sleepsuits make quite a pile, then there are gifts of clothes waiting to be worn, as well as outgrown garments. A wardrobe isn't essential. Instead, choose a generous chest with plenty of drawers, which can be updated with a coat of paint or contemporary handles. A giant laundry basket is a must for a fast turnover of clothes. Wicker baskets, zinc tubs or colourful plastic crates stacked on shelves or tucked beneath the cot will all make tidying easy.

Your baby's room needs to be no-nonsense, but it must be safe and cosy too. Anticipate the investigative crawling phase by keeping blind cords short, trailing cables clipped and plug covers on, with a high shelf for any out-of-bounds items, and bars or catches on the windows. If you have a wooden floor, add a rug for softness, or choose a good quality, plain wool carpet that cleans up well. Sisal and coir are a little too rough for soft knees. Just as you would with any room in the house, strive for the perfect ambience. Everyone should feel tranquil and calm in the nursery. You'll reap the reward of planning for simplicity: neither you nor your new baby knows quite yet what their favourite things will be.

rooms for girls

Little girls adore pink, but they love baby blue, dreamy lilac and grass green too. Give your daughter a clear, pretty canvas onto which she can stamp her personality with favourite things, and organize it sensibly, so it's easy for her to tidy.

2

THIS PAGE AND OPPOSITE:
Converted from a hallway in the basement of a Victorian house, Cordelia's bedroom is a triumph of clever space planning. The MDF bed is scaled down to fit the room's narrow proportions, yet still holds toy drawers beneath and a generous bookshelf at its foot. Behind the bedhead wall is a full-height cupboard. If a room needs more light and planning regulations permit, a new window adds novelty. At night, this one is shuttered with MDF discs. An all-white room needs a splash of bold colour for fun. Choose a small area and work through the colour wheel as years go by.

" I like the windows in my bedroom. They look like balloons! "

CORDELIA, AGE 4

Most little girls love pretty things. But give your daughter a break from the classic, flowery bedroom and instead provide her with a fresh, contemporary take on the look. Crisp fondant colours or an all white room provide the perfect background for little girls to display their special treasures. For tomboys, more muted shades and quirky, abstract patterns are appealing. Guard against reliving your own childhood fantasies on your daughter's territory. Just because you were denied shocking pink as a child doesn't mean she'll want it now.

If you're unsure where to pitch the style of the room, look to your daughter for inspiration. Amazingly, even a three-year-old will have strong opinions, so talk to your little girl about her favourite colours. If she's still too small, observe the things she's naturally attracted to. Does she reach for pink frilly dresses or a brightly coloured T-shirt? What colours does she choose when painting? These little clues can provide you with an excellent decorative starting point. Keep the details flexible, so that you can chop and change as the years go by. Painted walls rather than wallpaper, display space for treasured accessories and classic furniture all make for a relaxed, easy bedroom. Stick to simple styles and a streamlined layout, and the room will look effortlessly fresh and modern.

When a toddler turns two and graduates from a cot to a bed, it provides a timely moment for reassessing the bedroom and making stylistic changes. Focus first on the hard-working furniture, planning colours later. Basic pieces won't differ hugely from the baby years, but now a good bed becomes the central focus. Invest in the best mattress you can afford. Children may be light but they need firm support, and a good-quality mattress should last for ten years. Think long and hard about the style of bed you choose. Girls will go through myriad fads, from Barbie-doll fever at five to seriously sophisticated at ten. Work backwards. If a classic style with a contemporary twist seems suitable for a pre-teen, it can be made appropriately childlike for the earlier years.

Select a distinctive frame to make the bed a strong focal point and save boring divans for teenagers or spare bedrooms. Plain and simple reconditioned hospital beds look cosy for tiny children, especially when accessorized with a graphic animal-motif duvet or piled high with candy-coloured floral pillows for older girls. Self-assembly MDF sleigh beds are another versatile option. The high curved sides mean little ones can't fall out of bed, and the ready-to-paint frame can be reinvented in bubblegum pink then powder blue followed by hot orange as girly crazes wax and wane. If you only need a headboard, be inventive and customize one. In place of a traditional Goldilocks-style curved bedhead, choose a more contemporary rectangular shape, with cut-out circles or hearts. Think fairyland, think woodland grotto, and create a headboard from picket fencing or gold-painted wood adorned with giant faux gemstones.

Canopied and four-poster beds, bunk beds or sleeping platforms prove irresistible to girls, as well as providing extra space for sleepover friends. For adults, squeezed halfway up a tiny ladder trying to make the bed,

THIS PAGE AND OPPOSITE: With its patterned pillows, white walls and shutters, this five-year-old's bedroom strikes the right balance: it's pretty, yet not inappropriately boudoirish. Children adore whimsical touches, so scour junk shops for unusual buys. Here, the lighting includes teacup sconces (above left), an illuminated goose and a tiny dressmaker's dummy, while the bedside radio is a car (above right). Ready-to-paint MDF furniture (left) can be customized with simple motifs like dots, hearts and pretty colours. If a little girl has a large room, a double bed can offer a comforting oasis.

they may be marginally less popular. Yet you can have great fun designing a special bed. A simple wood or tubular metal four-poster affords plenty of decorative potential and looks very contemporary. Frames can be draped with brightly coloured net one year, home-made strings of shells the next, or with inexpensive, glittery sari silks for older girls. Or you could create a canopy with a plain mosquito net hand-sewn with fake flowers. A raised bed can usefully accommodate storage or a desk beneath, and for stylistic continuity can be custom-made in materials used elsewhere in the house. Practical plywood, painted MDF or galvanized steel are all options, and will be softened with colourful bed linen and teddies.

If you have decided on the bed, let your daughter make some choices too. Gradually amass a varied selection of bed linen so that as she gets older bedmaking becomes creative rather than a chore. Snap up odd sheets or pillowcases in department-store sales or hunt down flowery retro eiderdowns at junk shops or jumble sales. In the same way that little girls love to pick and choose their dolls' clothes, they'll relish the chance to mix and match pretty pillowcases and duvet covers. Provided they are from a complementary palette, crisp checks, plains and florals mixed with white will look wonderful jumbled together on the bed. Extras like an embroidered baby pillowcase, cosy travel blanket, or appliquéd top sheet make the final effect more individual. For a particularly modern bed, choose plain linens in a number of hot shades – perhaps a cerise pillowcase and duvet cover teamed with a lime bottom sheet. All white is no fun for a colour-conscious child, but if you're insistent at least customize a white duvet cover with a satin appliqué or button trim.

" *I love my bed, because it's nice and cosy. I keep lots of my special things up here.* **"**

LUCY, AGE 8

THIS PAGE AND OPPOSITE: With its funky materials – rubber floor, plywood bed and polypropylene chair – eight-year-old Lucy's bedroom also has the basics for a teenager's den. A series of plain, colourful surfaces creates a versatile canvas that can be dressed up with floral beanbags or kept simple for a tomboy. An entire wall covered in blackboard provides endless entertainment. A custom-made platform bed in painted MDF or plywood, as here, is not only a brilliant space-saver, but also creates a cosy, self-contained unit for a child.

THIS PAGE AND OPPOSITE: Girlish schemes need not be flowery: pale sugared-almond tones look equally feminine. In this seven-year-old's attic eyrie, eau-de-Nil walls, pastel bedding and butterflies do the trick. For a little girl who values privacy, create a hide-away. String suspension wire between walls to divide off the bed area, and add a voile curtain. 'Found' objects lend romance: here, a cabinet is home to an eclectic mix.

The bed may be top priority, but storage comes a close second. Plan for, or with, your daughter by writing an exhaustive list of everything she needs to keep in her bedroom, from toys and clothes to decorative inessentials. You will need flexible storage to accommodate a child's eclectic collection of possessions, which can range from masses of tiny toys to bigger items like a dolls' house. Not everything has to be put away at all times, but each item should have a home. It's simply not true that children are naturally messy. Most love to be tidy. It's up to you to provide sensible storage so clearing up is quick and easy.

Provided the room is large enough, the smartest and simplest storage option is to fit a run of cupboards with floor-to-ceiling, flush-fitting doors along one wall. Behind this façade you can provide a multitude of different-sized shelves, roomy enough to hold individual crates for small items yet deep enough for piles of sweaters and jeans, and including space for a hanging rail. Open shelves may seem a tempting option for finding toys at a glance, but closed doors are preferable. At bedtime you want the room to be peaceful, without a child's favourite toys temptingly on view. Once cupboard doors are shut it doesn't matter how messy things are inside. The doors can be as simple or as inspired as you like. Paint them the same colour as the wall and fit small handles positioned at child height,

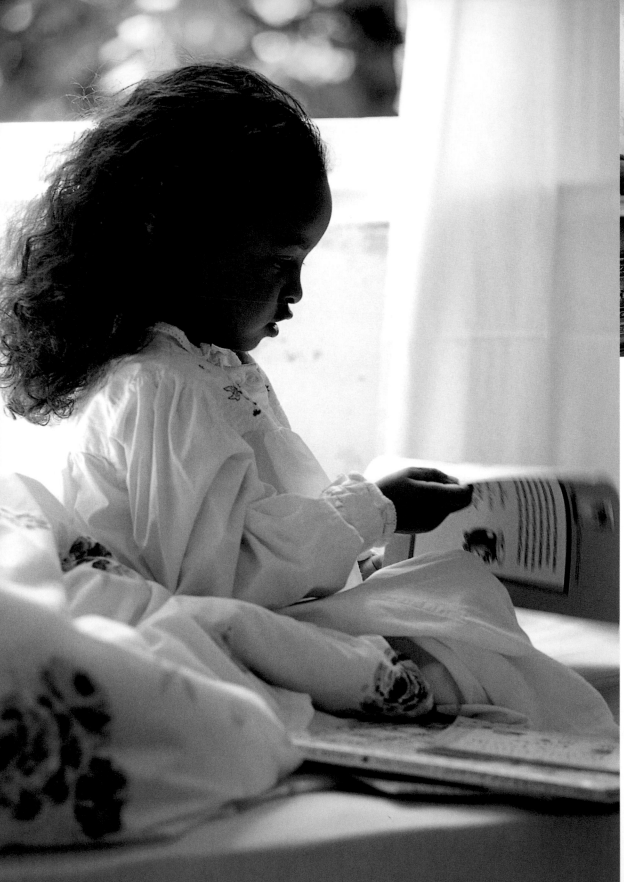

THIS PAGE AND OPPOSITE:
Many little girls love a heady mix of florals, and three-year-old Cyprus is no exception. Avoid over-co-ordinating floral patterns and add splashes of a primary colour, perhaps a scarlet pillow slip, to give essential bite to the sweeter pastels. Mixed with an iron bedstead and painted wooden furniture in strong shades, the look is fresh and modern rather than traditionally rustic. To focus attention on a floral bed, play down the rest of the decor, sticking to white walls and plain curtains, and add several pillows and cushions for a grown-up feel.

and they'll all but disappear. An eggshell finish provides an ideal surface to display artwork. Alternatively, you could make doors from Perspex, aluminium or plywood for a contemporary spin. If you are saddled with a chest of drawers that's practical but unattractive, site it in an alcove and fit it with modern, flush doors.

Ideally, you should provide an area for your little girl to draw and do her homework. Shop-bought dressing tables and desks are often frustratingly small and have fiddly detailing. Take a tip from contemporary interiors and provide her with a long, low worktop with wall-mounted shelves above. It could be painted MDF or covered in stainless steel or colourful laminate. Site the computer here; beneath the bench, fit crates on castors for toys or books, a second stool for a friend, even a cabinet with lots of shallow drawers for colouring pens and paper. If you add a mirror, a worktop can also double as a dressing table and display space. It's important for display areas to be comfortably within a little one's reach, not high up on a shelf. Don't be controlling about what she wants to show off. You may not appreciate a collection of glittery nail polish and papier mâché fruit, but beauty is in the eye of the beholder. She, in turn, will appreciate an arrangement of grown-up fresh flowers. Little bowls and baskets will keep hairclips, jewellery and nail-stickers in order.

Most children relish a colourful environment and will want to be involved in choosing their favourite shades. Painted walls are much more flexible than childish patterned wallpaper and provide a cleaner background for the inevitable jumble of toys. See what happens when you offer some paint colour charts to your little one. You may be amazed at her innate good taste and the shades she picks. Older girls will enjoy dipping into sample pots of several colours and painting large squares of cardboard to prop up against the walls while deciding on a shade. Follow the same colour rules as you would anywhere else in the house. Jolly brights like sherbet yellow or cornflower blue are stimulating, but use them on a single wall so the

In the same way that little girls love to pick and choose their dolls' clothes, they'll relish the chance to mix and match pretty pillowcases and duvet covers.

THIS PAGE AND OPPOSITE: **A four-poster lends instant glamour to a bedroom – perfect for pre-teens. A simple metal frame becomes dramatic and sophisticated when swathed with fabric – anything from pastel voile to sari silk – that has been hemmed and given a slot heading. Alternatively, try inexpensive shop-bought tab-top curtains that can be changed regularly. Choose grown-up plain bed linen, in white or bright plains. The rest of the bed frame can be dressed up with Chinese lanterns, faux flowers or a twist of fairy lights.**

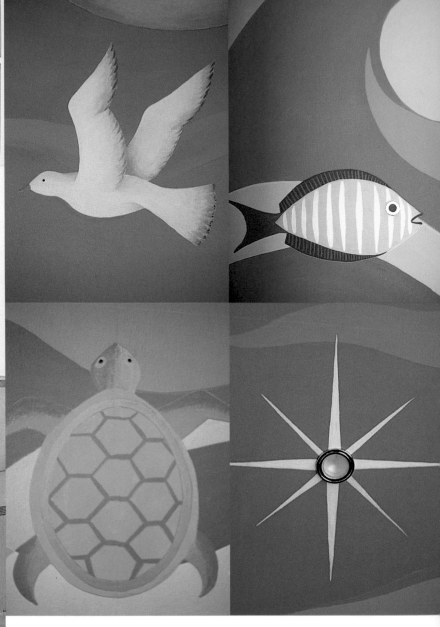

THIS PAGE AND OPPOSITE:
Both sexes will relish a
theme bedroom, and don't
assume girls will want a
fairy grotto. This little girl's
boat bed, with its seafaring
theme, has delighted her
since her toddler years.
Provided the painting is
professionally done, a full-
scale mural is the perfect
antidote to a nondescript
bedroom. Keep the images
bold, and consider
incorporating a shaped bed.
This bed is imaginative,
beautiful and practical: it
was custom-made for the
space, including storage
drawers below the steps.

effect isn't overpowering. If your daughter is dead set on a pastel and you're not, shift the tone a little to an off-pastel for a more sophisticated effect. Or suggest positive alternatives: substitute lilac for pink, or soft leafy green for the more usual pale yellow.

If you're set on a contemporary style, and your daughter wants an ultra-feminine retreat, it's still possible to tread a stylistic fine line between the two. An exuberant flowery fabric will please you both, provided it is tailored into a Roman blind instead of full curtains, and teamed with a simple aluminium bed frame and plain sheets. Alternatively, keep walls and windows simple, with white paint and white self-patterned voile, but choose floral bed linen. Butterfly or leaf motifs are good alternatives to flowers, or you can achieve a girly look by customizing a white blind with sequins and covering floor cushions in shell or eau-de-Nil satin. If you can't agree, and want to avoid making expensive mistakes, fit the window with a plain roller blind, simple metal pole and curtain clips. Style-conscious little girls can ring the curtain changes with anything from a length of Liberty Tana lawn to spotty voile. Cover the nursery armchair in cheap, washable white cotton duck and make cushions together. Citrus-coloured linens with a bright monogram, or pink denim with purple cross-stitch, will look trendy and smart.

Every little girl needs a space to display her artwork, photographs or poems on the wall. Conventional cork or padded pinboards are often too small. Much smarter is a large piece of steel, powder-coated in a shade to match the walls. Use magnets to attach drawings, pictures and cards, allowing displays to be changed frequently without stripping the paint from the walls. Glass clip-frames or painted wood frames arranged symmetrically are a smart way to display favourite photos or to create an informal family tree. Don't overlook the decorative potential of childish paintings. Imaginatively framed school artwork, with a bright mount, can turn a naïve illustration into stunning Pop Art.

Remember that good as you want your daughter's room to look, it is her own private haven, a place for chats with friends, somewhere quiet to do homework, a retreat for dreaming and scheming. Providing privacy for children is vital. Help your daughter to delineate her territory from other siblings so she can be alone when she chooses. You could mark her door with a giant gilded initial, or get a metalwork company to cut out her name in stainless-steel letters. Alternatively, she might enjoy hand-painting her monogram using special calligraphy. Agree on a more imaginative sign than a hand-scrawled 'Keep Out'. A necklace strung with colourful lettered beads and hung over the door handle is far prettier. Use ingenuity to provide her with a cubbyhole for secret things. If replastering is on the agenda, could a small alcove be inset into the wall? Perhaps a tiny built-in cupboard could be set into a boarded-up fireplace?

Bedrooms should be fun, so indulge in a smattering of kitsch. Search funky shops for little extras: a beaded curtain to hang over the doorway, a glitter ball to spin from the ceiling, giant fake flowers, a leopard-print cushion. Most mothers are still little girls at heart. If you like something, the chances are your daughter will too.

rooms for boys

For boys, create a cool den that's fuss-free and has versatile furniture for imaginative play. Raid the colour spectrum for inspiration – scarlet, leaf green, indigo – then team with robust surfaces like rubber and wood so no-one worries about the inevitable scrapes and dents.

3

THIS PAGE AND OPPOSITE: **Very little boys need a tranquil atmosphere and plenty of tactile textures to promote a safe, cosy feel. In two-year-old Flinn's bedroom, a high picket-fence headboard, faux-fur rug and thick, tufted curtains do the trick. In a room with lots of natural daylight, heavy interlined curtains like these ones are very useful for cutting out glare. The basic elements for surfaces and windows can be culled from grown-up decorating, then made jolly and childlike with pictures, details and accessories. Here, storage is not only practical but also lots of fun: a bookshelf loaded with colourful Ladybird books (above left) and a collection of little shoes haphazardly piled high (above) create plenty of contrast to the peaceful white paint.**

Boys care passionately about their bedrooms. From around five years old, most know instinctively what accessories and motifs are 'cool' and will want to incorporate at least some into their private space. They may fuss less than girls about an overall scheme, but are obsessive when it comes to the smaller details. What boys need most is empty floor space – as much as you can spare – and plenty of storage so that their myriad collections, from toy soldiers to racing cars, can stay sorted and ready for play. Furniture that offers a bit of action – ladders to climb, platforms to scoot along – goes down a storm, too.

It may sound sexist, but rule number one is that everything in a boy's room should be robust. When play gets rowdy, he won't think twice about bashing the bedhead: plan for that from the toddler years, and everyone can relax. Therefore a wall-mounted, enamel-shaded bedside lamp is a more sensible option than a fragile Japanese paper one, and a sturdy metal sports locker more practical than a canvas beach-hut wardrobe. Imagine each piece of furniture being jumped off, climbed on or moved around as part of a pirate ship game or impromptu kickabout, and you'll get a realistic picture. With this in mind,

Little boys need efficient, well-planned storage to help keep their things in order. For toys, the ideal storage system combines plenty of small drawers, crates or boxes for compartmentalizing tiny toys with bookshelves and perhaps taller storage space for larger items.

LEFT: **If space is tight, then choose a single, all-purpose piece of furniture, with drawers for clothes, shelves for books and a spacious top that can double as a display area for treasured possessions. Coats and shirts are easily hung on wall hooks. The bedroom is the ideal place to display a child's artwork, so fit one wall with a giant pinboard.**

" *I like my room because it's clean and tidy.*" FLINN, AGE 2½

it makes sense to pick scratch-resistant modern materials like laminate and plywood, or painted furniture that can be easily touched up with a lick of paint.

In a boy's room too, the bed will be the central focus. Why not take that literally, and situate it in the middle of the room: a bunk bed is much easier to turn into an imaginary ship or climbing frame if it's easy to get at. In terms of changing tastes and needs, boys have a steeper developmental curve than girls. They still require a cosy sleeping nook at the age of three, but by five are ready for a more adventurous, classically boyish option. There are alternatives for tackling such shifting criteria. Either buy a generously sized cot bed for the baby stage, and get a serious boy's bed once your son outgrows the cot. Or invest in a grown-up bed at the age of two, and make it inviting with a jolly duvet and accessories for the early years. A bunk bed is an excellent option. Your son can sleep on the safe lower level until about the age of six, and graduate to the higher level when he feels ready.

Boys, as much as girls, appreciate a fuss being made over their bed. It does not simply represent somewhere to sleep, but is a child's special safe and secure zone as well as being a potential platform for imaginative games. Ready-to-buy modern options might include sophisticated dark wood or painted *bateau lit* and sleigh bed frames, simple iron bedsteads, colourful melamine platform beds with storage drawers, or sturdy tubular metal and canvas army-camp styles. You'll get the best fun and most individual results by dreaming up a customized bed. In an attic, a built-in MDF bed can be slotted in beneath sloping eaves, with roomy pull-out drawers beneath, all faced in tongue-and-groove. For an older boy, a simple plywood platform becomes something special and looks modern when supported on giant castors or sophisticated tubular metal legs. Alternatively, you could commission a carpenter to build a boat or a spaceship pod around a standard divan. A theme bed can look stunning, provided the rest of the decoration in the room is simple and clean-lined.

BELOW: **A child-size washbasin, perhaps a small cloakroom model, is a boon in the bedroom – great for encouraging teeth-brushing. Cross-head taps are easiest for little fingers to turn. This is also an ideal spot to site a medicine cabinet to hold child-related basics from Calpol to thermometers but hang it high on the wall and make sure it is lockable with a stiff key.**

BELOW RIGHT: **In Flinn's bedroom, a curtained alcove provides additional storage space. If a proper wardrobe threatens to dominate a small bedroom, this is a good way to conceal toys and out-of-season clothes.**

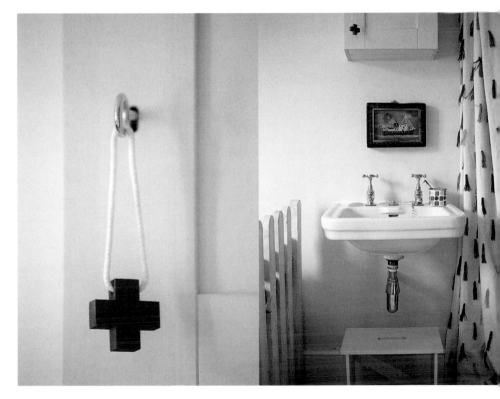

THIS PAGE AND OPPOSITE:
Instead of traditional sludgy
shades, choose quirky,
vibrant colours for a trendy,
bright boy's room like eight-
year-old Gabriel's. A bold
palette also provides a
cheery antidote to khaki
army toys and black plastic
gadgets. Encourage boys
to get creative with the
paintbrush and pick out
special details – freehand
splotches around the light
switches or panels of
contrasting colour on the
inside of the door frame or
the backs of shelves.

Floorboards can be coated
in a tough, glossy floor paint
for a practical finish. In a
small room, a bunk bed
(even if the child doesn't
share) is a great idea, acting
as a chill-out area and
climbing frame as well as a
sleepover space for friends.
A custom-made desk shaped
from MDF is more fun than
a traditional design. Wall-
mount as much furniture as
possible, leaving space for
all the essentials of the boy
zone – a football table,
punchbag, dartboard or
basketball hoop.

For most boys past the age of five, a bunk bed or raised sleeping platform is a dream option. These days a number of shops stock tubular metal bunk beds, which are infinitely more stylish than the varnished pine variety. If you'd prefer to build a platform bed, a mix of modern materials like stainless steel, plywood, beech or painted MDF are all good options. Think about safety and access. There should be a decent guard rail along the open side of the bed; one that a little body can't wriggle through in the midst of a restless dream. Yet make the bed sufficiently accessible that it's still possible to tuck in sheets and blankets properly. To climb up, a ladder is the most conventional choice, but make sure it's fixed securely in place. Metal rungs firmly attached to the supporting wall beneath or beside the bed also look good. If there's room, a staircase created from giant building blocks is an imaginative way up to bed. Boys appreciate little extras, including mini-slides, rope ladders or clip-on ramps (perfect to join up two bunk beds if boys are sharing). Tie-on canvas or sailcloth panels are also good for imaginative play.

A raised bed frees up more floor space for playing, so is a boon in a small room. Storage cupboards, a generous run of worktop or, with a lower bed, lots of pull-out drawers, can be variously incorporated underneath. Whatever bed you choose, when planning the remaining bedroom furniture try to find slim, streamlined pieces that don't encroach on valuable floor space, or movable items that can be pushed up against the wall during energetic games. Make furniture on castors a theme – everything from a chest of drawers to a low play table. Even better, clear the floor with wall-mounted shelves for books, baskets for miscellaneous bits and pieces, hooks for clothes and even ceiling-suspended seating – perhaps a hammock or a swinging pod chair.

Little boys need efficient, well-planned storage to help keep their things in order. Most boys have minimal interest in clothes and in putting them away, so devise a simple storage system. Open shelves in a cupboard are the easiest option, but clearly label each section for T-shirts,

66 *I like my bed because I can sleep on the top bunk. Sometimes a friend stays over and sleeps underneath. The colours are great because they really make my room stand out.* **99**

GABRIEL, AGE 8

jeans and so on. Alternatively, build a series of box-shaped cupboards at child height all around the room, with each one devoted to a certain category of clothing, and fitted with a different-coloured MDF or stainless-steel door to resemble a sports locker. The top of the cupboards can be used for sports trophies or toy display. A hanging rail isn't a priority. Instead, give your son a long row of child-height hooks where he can hang up his pyjamas or anything else that has been strewn across the floor. Don't expect him to line up his boots and shoes neatly. Instead, provide one big basket, and agree that this is the designated place for all shoes at tidy-up time.

The older a child gets, the more time he'll spend playing in his room. For toys, the ideal storage system combines plenty of small crates or boxes for compartmentalizing little things (cars, Lego, plastic animals), bookshelves, and perhaps taller storage spaces for larger items like a pop-up tent or sports equipment. Settling down to play is much less enticing if toys are in a muddle, and most children are intensely appreciative of a freshly sorted-out bedroom. A simple wood or melamine unit, with alcoves for slotting in toy

BELOW: **An antique dark wood bed will grow up with its owner. Here, the look is prevented from becoming too adult by a quirky mix of accessories: a giraffe-print side table, flag-emblazoned wall and checked and patchwork bedding.**

crates, is a very sensible option, and looks cool and modern when fitted with crates painted in a rainbow of funky colours. If you have the budget, look in contemporary furniture stores for dayglo polypropylene pieces – drawer units on castors, for example, or folding tables – all of which provide trendy, versatile storage that will grow with your child. If space is in short supply, giant shallow boxes on wheels can be built to slide under the bed, though they should be fitted with plenty of dividers.

Indulge your little boy's passion for complex structures, be it Lego or a toy castle, and give him a proper surface for displaying them. The floor is never the best place because special treasures will have to be removed for cleaning. Instead, provide a low table and instruct everyone, from the au pair to younger siblings, that this is no-go territory. Cover the tabletop in something indestructible, like stainless steel or oilcloth, so that it doesn't matter if there are glue spills or paint splodges while craft-making is in progress. In addition, little boys need a desk or computer table for working at, complete with task lighting and a good chair: there are plenty of groovy metal or coloured-plastic swivel seats

BELOW: **Some boys like their bedrooms to be uncluttered and no-nonsense. Brighten the army camp look with a few outrageous touches. The green rubber floor, giant Stars and Stripes and cowhide rug make this room as cool as a teenager's den.**

THIS PAGE AND OPPOSITE: Brilliant, saturated colour on every surface, from walls to furniture, turns an ordinary bedroom into an entertaining playroom, usually the best option if a boy has a large, sunny room. Don't stop with the walls: paint skirting boards, cupboard doors, the bed and bookcase, all in vivid Smartie shades. Dark floorboards will balance the vivid colour, while a cotton rug makes for comfortable floor play. In this five-year-old's room, the startling walls are matched by equally vibrant bed linen – a riot of crazy stripes, animals and exotic fruits.

in the shops. Also give him a display area that can be devoted to treasures like christening gifts, home-made models and toy cars. A thick MDF shelf fixed above the bed, perhaps painted in a bold colour, or a stainless-steel catering shelf rack for older boys, make great choices.

Little boys play constantly on the floor, so flooring should be hard-wearing and attractive as well as providing a smooth surface. There's nothing more frustrating than trying to race cars along badly sanded wooden boards, or to arrange army platoons on bumpy sisal matting. Far more practical, and infinitely smarter, are painted or waxed wooden boards, wood laminate flooring or brightly coloured rubber tiles. Wooden boards needn't be left in their natural colour: they could be graphically painted with roads, grass verges and rooftops for a car fanatic, or in startling purple gloss with yellow planets for a space fan. Boys still appreciate comfort, so do add a rug as well. You could choose a grown-up abstract design in jolly colours that the kids will appreciate too. Some children's mail-order catalogues stock dual-purpose rugs with snakes and ladders or hopscotch designs, which can be both played with and sat upon. A rug could even be the starting point for a simple decorative theme: a zebra print inspiring a *Jungle Book* mood complete with a fake leopard throw on the bed, or a groovy fake-grass rug for a tractor and farmyard fanatic.

Though they'll respond instinctively to colour and pattern, little chaps generally show less interest than girls when asked to select a favourite paint shade or decorative theme. Don't force them: instead, whitewash the walls and inject splashes of contemporary colour; anything from a broad-striped scarlet and white duvet cover to a giant orange felt pinboard or lime and indigo denim beanbags. They'll soon tell you if the colours don't suit. If plain walls are too boring, there are plenty of quirky ways to decorate. One wall draped from floor to ceiling with a giant flag looks bold and stylish. Alternatively, line the walls with colourful maps, fit a floor-to-ceiling blackboard for boys to

Give your little boy a display area that can be devoted to treasures like christening gifts, home-made models and toy cars. A thick MDF shelf fixed above the bed and painted in a bold colour is a great choice.

THIS PAGE AND OPPOSITE: Detailing counts for just as much in a child's bedroom as it does in a grown-up space. Ornaments should be colourful and fun, though many children do like to display more formal christening gifts. Give boys plenty of space to show off their funny papier mâché 'makes' and treasures. A shelf unit (opposite) can be the decorative centrepiece of a room. It needn't always be immaculately tidy: you'll learn to appreciate the innate, chaotic charm of kids' mess! Children love anything that spells out their name. Letters on the door (below left) lend an air of importance, as does anything monogrammed.

scrawl on, or use a metallic silver wallpaper (great as a background for space paintings). Carefully chosen, large props mounted on the wall will also look modern against a single bright colour. What about a boogie board, a giant fishing net threaded with plastic fish, or a series of large plastic dinosaurs creeping across the ceiling?

If your little one is mad about a cartoon character, be it Bob the Builder or Batman, indulge their passion with a giant floor cushion made up in appropriate fabric, or an enormous poster, then ignore further demands. Crazes come and go, and next year your little boy will have moved on to another phase. A generic theme, subtly done, is much more enduring and gives you a decorative 'hook' as a starting point. Create a neutral canvas with plain painted walls and a white roller blind, then you can introduce all manner of different themes. Kitted out with a green rubber floor, cowhide-patterned furniture and a blue ceiling, the bedroom becomes a farmyard retreat. With timber decking, porthole-shaped windows and a boat-print duvet cover, he'll be at sea exploring every night. Whatever theme you choose, ensure the key elements are inexpensive and easy to change.

OPPOSITE: **This toddler's bedroom has been created from a sectioned-off area of loft. The plywood storage unit acts as a divider between the room and the living space where, on the reverse of the unit, books are housed. Tall ceilings can feel impersonal, but by enclosing the bed with high sides, a cosy corner has been created for a little boy.**
LEFT: **Kids adore sleeping in nooks and crannies, so don't automatically turn the space beneath the eaves into a wardrobe. A built-in bed might be more fun. Work with the shapes you have: here, a bookcase is part of the design, but extra space might instead be used to create a secret cupboard.**

THIS PAGE AND OPPOSITE:
A platform bed is a marvellous space-saver, particularly in a narrow room. In this seven-year-old's bedroom, raising the bed off the ground has freed up the floor area for play, and created space for clothes and toy storage cupboards on either side of the doorway. The generous

bookcases are wall hung so as not to impede play space. This room deftly demonstrates how to reinterpret the classic boys' theme – boats – without covering everything in motifs. With its round windows, decking-effect beech boards and metal bed rail, a yacht springs instantly to mind.

Boys may be boisterous and busy, but there are times when they want a special area in their bedroom for relaxing and being with friends. If there's no room for a sofa, give your little boy the chance to turn his bed into a lounge-lizard spot. He will enjoy touchy-feely fabrics on the bed. Keep duvet covers and sheets in strong plains (T-shirt jersey bedding is a good texture) and add a pure wool checked blanket. A giant fleece-fabric blanket in a vivid hue like scarlet or grass green looks neat tucked over the duvet by day. A cut-up old sleeping bag, made into squishy cushions, is also fun. Give boys the chance to create their own ambience in the room using lighting. A bubble lamp by the bed, a light-up globe on the desk or a funky coil of lights are all good options. Try to squeeze in a few quirky additions. A football table, punchbag or wall-hung basketball hoop will make your son's room the coolest den he could ask for.

❝ I love climbing up the ladder to go to bed. It's a special place up there. ❞

CHRISTY, AGE 7

shared

rooms

Siblings who share need clearly marked personal zones, their own private corners and decoration they both adore. Kit out their room with two of everything, then create a fun environment that's ideal for shared play and midnight feasts, yet serene enough for soothing bedtimes.

4

Plenty of children share a bedroom. As a parent, you may anticipate only the downsides: disrupted bedtimes, arguments over territory, one child wanting to study while the other chooses to chat. But it needn't be a nightmare. Ask any grown-up who shared a room to recall childhood memories, and many will fondly remember the fun of reading by torchlight after lights-out or the pleasure of two sets of toys. Besides, for a child to wake up with his siblings and fall asleep with them each night is a great gift. Approach decorating a shared bedroom with confidence, and the results will be fun for everyone. Younger siblings may even be fighting to squeeze in.

Demarcation of territory is crucially important. From an early age, children love to have personal space where they can keep their special treasures and retreat with toys or friends. If your kids are small, it's your job to decide who has what space, but with older children include them in the conversation. Start with a floor plan and move around scaled-down cut-out pieces of furniture that need to be incorporated to see what works well and looks good where. If the room has great proportions and two windows, the most sensible option is to split it down the middle. It's more likely that allocating the space will include some compromises, and divisions may not be equal in terms of square metres. Try to compensate fairly. If one child gets the window, give the other the mantelpiece for display.

Kids will find it fun (and you will find it politic) to have a formal division of territory, so that during arguments or when entertaining friends each can retreat to their private zone. First, decide if the division will be visual or physical. For little ones, the less physical separation the better. They will derive comfort at night by having their beds close together, and reading a joint story will be simpler for you. It might be amusing to divide the room with a brightly painted line of coloured footprints or chunky arrows on the wall or on a wooden floor. Older siblings will relish imaginative solutions that section off the bedroom. Consider a plasterboard wall with cut-out portholes so the

THIS PAGE AND OPPOSITE: **One way to approach a boy-plus-girl shared room is to keep the basics unisex. In this room, shared by a three-year-old girl and seven-year-old boy, polished boards, metal cupboards and identical metal-legged beds provide a neutral background. Give each child's area a distinct** character by using the bed and wall behind it as a focal point. Paint it in hot pinks and oranges for a girl and in muted tones for a boy. Think about the layout: would the kids prefer to sleep at opposite ends of the room or side by side? And, where there is shared furniture, it's important for both to have ease of access.

THIS PAGE AND OPPOSITE: An individual wall display by each child's bed is a good way to delineate territory. Here, boldly coloured walls are a stunning background for an assortment of objects – tiny dolls' clothes, pictures and photographs. Start off a creative mix on the child's behalf, then encourage them to add to the collection. Retro furniture is ideal for kids' rooms. If a piece is not in pristine condition, it doesn't matter if it gets the odd knock, and furniture may come in wild colours with practical wipe-clean laminate surfaces.

kids can still chat, or a floor-to-ceiling sliding MDF screen. Boys might enjoy individual custom-made screens in hole-punched steel that they can wheel to the end of the bed; girls could have four-poster beds draped with a length of voile or organza for privacy.

If your children get on well, divide up the room space into separate sleeping, play and work zones instead of two distinct areas with bed, chest and so on. This is the most sensible option for older children or if space is restricted. Bunk beds or sleeping pods on a shared platform can be divided from the play space with a sliding screen or floor-to-ceiling sheer curtains. The children can either share one long countertop to do their homework, or have two identical desks side by side. If older kids find that concentration is a problem, put up a plywood screen between them, and it can double as a pinboard. The remaining floor area can be devoted to games, and there's no further need for a playroom.

When a boy and a girl share, your most pressing problem will be how to marry two definite and probably wildly differing tastes. For little ones, paint the walls white or choose a bold shade, then concentrate on personalizing each child's bed. There's nothing more charming than two identical bedsteads side by side, but characterize each with different duvet covers: an identical design, perhaps, but in two contrasting colours. Take the theme a step further, and colour co-ordinate each child's bedside table, rug and lampshade. If the children share bunks, individuality is even more essential. Personalize each level with favourite toys and cosy cushions. Alternatively, keep the look co-ordinated by having differently patterned duvets but in toning shades.

When it comes to wall colour, older siblings will have fun poring over paint charts to find a hue both can agree on. Provided shades are tonally harmonious, the most extraordinary selection can be combined, and the

look will still be confident and modern. For a cohesive scheme, select three shades. Use one for the girl's bedhead wall and another for the boy's bedhead wall. A neutral shade works well with brights, so if your daughter wants shocking pink and your son is into army fatigues give him a strong khaki. The third shade can be introduced in the form of upholstery on one side of the room, and picture mounts on the other. Painting all four walls in contrasting hues sounds outrageous, but combined with white duvets and a wooden floor it can look fabulous.

Kids' varied tastes in pattern are harder to resolve. A safe bet is to stick to checks, stripes or spots, but if little girls want something floral, an abstract flower-print duvet cover will sit well with, for example, a boy's car silhouette. Alternatively, a colourful fantasy mural will appeal to both sexes, but try to keep shapes simple and the look graphic.

66 *I love my room because it has my name all over the place. And I love the bookshelf. Now I don't have to keep my books under the bed.* 99

GEORGIA, AGE 6

In a shared all-girls room, decorative details can be a little more indulgent. Both girls may clamour for pink, but cooler shades, perhaps soft blue or faded red, still look pretty and sophisticated. If both girls love the overall scheme, most elements can be kept pleasingly identical. Here, the symmetry of side-by-side sleigh beds and twin chairs creates a tranquil ambience. Rigorously divide up the best elements of the room: here, one child has the skylight view while the other gets to turn the lamp off. Wooden letters on the wall (opposite) are a subtle way to mark out boundaries.

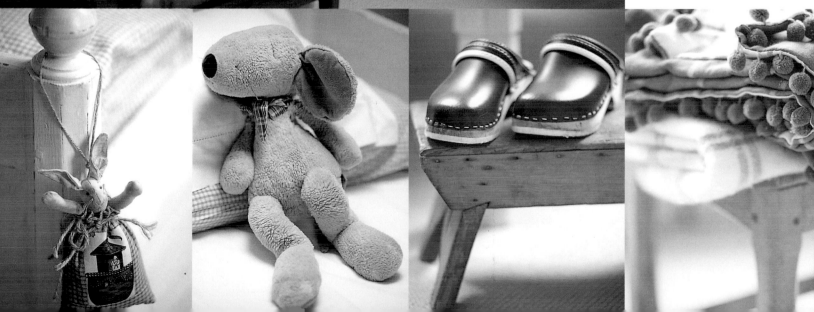

THIS PAGE AND OPPOSITE: One neat way to sidestep the issue of children with differing tastes is to dominate a bedroom with a fabulous mural. Somehow it negates the need for boundaries, because the room becomes a separate entity, everyone's room, a magical place to go to sleep and wake up in. A mural is a clever way to disguise awkward dimensions: in Millie, Florence and Isabel's bedroom, the tree shape was inspired by the chimney breast. Use the mural to inject an element of fantasy. Who will care about sharing a shelf when everyone can stack books on a tree branch?

> **" *My sister Sophie and I talk after lights-out and plot midnight feasts.* "** JACK, AGE 7

Generic themes usually make the best choices simply because they won't date too quickly. Properly painted, a woodland grotto, summer sky or moonscape can transform a plain bedroom. Remember that kids adore tiny details. Two giant green leaves painted on a white wall and crowded with red and black aphids will keep them amused for many bedtimes. Keep the remaining details simple. Plain, understated window treatments and duvets, simple bedsteads and contemporary wood or rubber flooring will take the edge off an overly cute visual appeal. Think how you might incorporate imaginative lighting into the mural. Twinkling wall lights emerging from a faux boat mast or starry sky are quite magical for little kids on the brink of sleep.

When same-sex siblings are sharing, you can easily indulge all-girl fantasies or all-boy passions. But you still need to personalize the two-of-everything accessories, so that sharers are clear about who owns what. You might want to keep the theme subtle with colour-coding: pink for one child's furniture and toy boxes, green for the other's. Bedding, laundry bags, lampshades and loose-covered chairs can all be individualized with a giant monogram, or allot each child a motif – perhaps a car for one, a butterfly for the other – which each can easily recognize as his or her own. Individual display areas, for everything from stones from the beach to photographs or framed certificates, and a section of wall or pinboard for personal artwork, are absolutely essential.

THIS PAGE: **Two divans placed at right angles, with a shared, sturdy cube side table, is a comforting and sensible option for little children. For Molly and Eli, there is no danger of knocking over furniture, and they can chat in bed while retaining a little privacy. In a shared room, good storage** is essential, so consider below-bed toy drawers and low divans that can double as a daytime sofa.

OPPOSITE: **Sharing a bedroom is about fun, so it's a sound investment to custom-build a giant platform that can sleep two, or hold one mattress with a play area at the other end.**

Some children are messy, while others are pin-neat, so to avoid arguments over tidying give each child his or her own chest of drawers, shelves or wardrobe. A bedside table for each, to hold a night-time drink, books and lamp, is also essential. Don't attempt to separate toy storage: if children are sharing a bedroom, then it makes sense for toys to be communal. It's a good idea to provide a few lidded crates for each child, however, so special toys like Barbie dolls or Pokémon cards can be kept well out of the way of inquisitive small siblings. Because shared bedrooms frequently double up as playrooms, ensure that everything can be tidied away quickly and hidden behind closed doors. Bedtime with two excitable children is stressful enough without a jumble of tempting toys peeping out from wicker baskets.

If you've picked a stimulating decorative scheme, flexible lighting is one way to calm things down at bedtime. In shared rooms, the correct lighting becomes even more important. Different-aged children may have staggered lights-out times, so that while an older child needs a well-shaded task light for reading in bed, his younger sibling might require a glowing nightlight. For playtime, low-voltage ceiling lights give brighter

THIS PAGE AND OPPOSITE: Offered the chance of bunk beds, most brothers will jump at the chance of sharing, though you can expect inevitable arguments about who gets the top bunk. This room for older boys takes a shared dormitory as its theme. White shutters, no-nonsense floorboards and utilitarian metal-framed beds all suggest summer camp, while the furniture – a battered sports locker, individual initialled trunks and aluminium chairs – completes the look. If dorm-style is your chosen theme, shared clothes storage and identical bedding are all part of the fun.

illumination than a single overhead pendant, but fit them with a dimmer switch for night-time. Consider a wacky lighting feature that both kids will enjoy. A giant clock, light-projected onto the wall, or an illuminated fish tank, would both look stunning.

When children enjoy sharing a bedroom, it becomes a real den, their own private space versus the family house, and a brilliant place to chill out. If space permits, give them a daybed, a child-size chaise longue, or an inflatable chair to lounge on, and consider installing a TV for older kids. If there is a younger sibling who doesn't share, and everyone is in agreement, the daybed (or a put-up bed) could be used at weekends for sleepovers so the little one can join in the fun. Likewise, give each child who shares the chance to sleep on his or her own occasionally, in a spare bedroom or on the sofabed. Children, like adults, occasionally need time out from the fray.

" *I like sharing. But Bo kicks my bed!* "

TUCKER, AGE 11

bath rooms

Plan a practical yet imaginative bathroom so the kids' daily ablutions are fun. Aim for a family bathroom that's sophisticated enough for grown-ups but suitable for children, too. Flexible storage and neutral shades are the keys to success.

5

The bathroom is one of the most hard-working spaces in the house. It needs to be efficient enough for the before-school wash and brush-up yet cosy enough to prompt fun-filled bathtimes. In terms of encouraging washing routines, you've won half the battle if the bathroom is a tempting place to spend time. Most children have a love–hate relationship with their daily ablutions. One week, they will obsessively brush their teeth; the next, they're terrified of the shower. But nearly all little ones find bathing soothing. Around the age of seven, children may choose not to bathe with siblings. Girls prefer splashing around with lotions and potions, while boys would rather be anywhere than in the bathroom.

If it's possible, give the children their own bathroom, which can also be used by guests. A designated kids' bathroom means you can install splashproof materials, scaled-down sanitaryware and jolly colours, and save more sophisticated details for your own bathroom. But if the room is really tiny, consider other options. Would you be better off creating a family-size bathroom elsewhere, with space for a large bath plus comfy chair? Would the tiny room work better as a toilet and basin, rather than trying to squeeze in a bath as well? Depending on the layout of the house, it might make sense for you to sacrifice your planned *en suite* bathroom to the family and have a tiny *en suite* shower room instead. Site the kids' bathroom close to their bedrooms. Slippery, tired children make bathtime chaotic enough, so the nearer they are to their pyjamas the better.

If you're planning a bathroom from scratch, firstly decide whether to have a bath and separate shower cubicle, or a wall-mounted shower attachment over the bath. Little ones generally prefer baths to showers. Many find the pressure of a power-shower uncomfortable on their heads, and they may be frightened by the rushing water. However, children are more likely to slip when they shower standing up in the bath.

THIS PAGE AND OPPOSITE:
A shared family bathroom has to please everyone, and with its zingy grapefruit colour scheme and glass skylights, this one does the trick. Always devote as much space as possible to the bathroom, then combine with an invigorating colour scheme and lots of light.

Good storage is essential, too. In this bathroom, there are under-sink cupboards as well as out-of-reach units for grown-up toiletries. The double basins are ideal for the morning rush. Adding a built-in nappy changing area is a nifty idea, though locate shelving for all the kit within arm's reach.

THIS PAGE AND OPPOSITE:
Bathtime is much more fun
for kids if there are
decorative touches that
appeal to their imagination.
But if a bathroom is shared
with adults, you can't allow
kids' stuff to take over. The
answer is to keep the decor
plain, using white tiles or
tongue-and-groove panelling,
so that the style easily
reverts to a grown-up mood.
Essential details include
a waterproof toy basket
and low shelves for the
children's bubble bath.
A wacky shower curtain
is a great way to inject fun:
shimmery silver, 3D flowers
or pockets for family snaps
are all good. Any extras will
be appreciated, from a
funky bathroom cabinet to
a fully fitted fish tank.

Children love to be independent, and being able to climb in and out of the bath by themselves is a milestone. But if the children's bathroom is to be shared with guests, spare a thought for an adult trying to squeeze into a tiny tub, and think twice before choosing a low, small bath.

If an over-bath shower is the only option, buy a non slip rubber mat and a groovy plastic shower curtain. Probably the best bath/shower configuration is to site a grown-up power-shower elsewhere in the house (perhaps in the utility room), and fit the children's bath with a hand-held shower attachment for washing hair.

Children love to be independent, and being able to climb in and out of the bath by themselves is a milestone. But if the children's bathroom is to be shared with guests, spare a thought for an adult trying to squeeze into a tiny tub and think twice before choosing a low, small bath. A big bath has lots of advantages. When siblings bathe together, they appreciate plenty of space for play, while in a family bathroom a generous bath will give you a share of adult luxury. Remember, fixing taps in the centre of a bath means neither child has to have the tap end.

To cope with the early morning rush, two (or even three) basins make sense. A row of scaled-down basins looks eye-catching, and is a sensible option if space is tight. There are plenty of stylish, practical choices that are ideal for kids. Small stainless-steel bowls set into a stone or wood worktop look ultra-trendy, as do wall-hung white ceramic butler's sinks. A small basin designed for cloakroom use is another option. The appeal of a wall-hung or inset basin is that you can lower the height for kids. For standard-size pedestal sinks, provide a sturdy plastic or wooden stool so children can step up to the correct height.

Little details will give small children the confidence they need to use the bathroom alone. Cross-head or lever taps are much easier to handle than slippery, minimal

LEFT AND ABOVE LEFT: **In a kids-only bathroom, fitting a small low-level bath and mini-washbasin is an appealing option. Roll-top baths are especially appropriate for children, as there are no sharp edges to bang little heads on. In this bathroom, three-year-old Cyprus is able to be almost entirely independent. Reconditioned Victorian baths are often a good option, as many come in small sizes. Consider having a central bath: it makes getting in and out easier, and there is also less likelihood of the walls getting splashed.**

round knobs, while a mixer tap will guard against scalds from the hot tap. Wall-mounted taps are easier to keep clean than basin-fitted ones. A counter with an inset washbasin provides ample space for washroom essentials. But if the basin is freestanding, fit the tooth mug into a wall-mounted holder, so it can't be knocked over, and replace slippery soap bars with liquid soap in a neat chrome dispenser. Think about the toilet. A wall-hung model can be sited slightly lower down. Is the handle too stiff for little fingers to flush? Would a push-button mechanism be better? If you have room, install a generously sized heated towel rail. There's nothing worse than being enfolded in yesterday's damp towel.

Make your bathroom one hundred per cent splashproof now, and you won't mind about water fights later. Fun floor options include non-slip rubber tiles in bright colours as well as linoleum and vinyl. Cork floor tiles with PVC laminate finish also come in water-themed designs such as sand and shells. Sealed or painted wooden boards are also suitable, though wood laminates are sensitive to deluges of bath water. Stone, such as limestone or slate, is smart, waterproof and, if you install underfloor heating, feels fabulous underfoot. However, it does get slippery when wet, so invest in a cosy absorbent bath mat. Children will also adore a concrete floor studded with pebbles and little shells, which also has plenty of grip.

ABOVE: **Small details, such as a brightly coloured toilet seat, can transform a small white bathroom, as will colourful towels.**
RIGHT: **Surfaces must be robust and easy to clean. Vividly coloured laminates make good bath panels and surrounds, while stone, from slate to marble, doesn't have to be reserved for adults – it's practical as well as stylish.**
OPPOSITE: **The ultimate luxury of a kids-only bathroom is that little sinks can be situated at child, not adult, height. Don't forget to include a stool for adults to perch on while supervising bathtime.**

THIS PAGE: **In a bathroom shared by adults and kids, a deep cast-iron bath adds a sense of luxury and is great to wallow in. If planning a shower, install an outsize shower tray, or build a 'wet' shower, so all the kids can squeeze in together. If fitting a power-shower, choose a shower head with the option for a gentler spray.**

OPPOSITE: **If space allows, double basins make perfect sense in a shared bathroom. Provide steps so little ones, like five-year-old Gussie, can reach the basin. Allocate one basin to the children, with a shelf for toothbrushes and novelty soaps, then gather more sophisticated 'grown-up' toiletries around the other.**

The walls will get splashed with lots of water so floor-to-ceiling tiles are sensible. In a kids-only bathroom, big, square tiles in a cheerful shade look graphic and modern. For a co-ordinated look, colour-match them with a painted wooden floor or laminate worktops. In a shared family bathroom, subway-style white brick tiles create a more sophisticated look, but work just as well with colourful bath toys as with adult accessories. Limestone-clad walls are another grown-up option, but resist glass and stainless-steel splashbacks. They may look chic, but will show every water mark. Laminates, which come in a host of enticing colours, are another good choice for bath panels and cupboard doors beneath vanity units.

Walls can also be lined with tongue-and-groove or MDF panels. Paint them and the walls in eggshell, which resists splash marks and condensation well. If sanitaryware is white, have fun with colour on the walls. Jazzy shades such as grass green and turquoise are particularly appropriate. Paint broad horizontal stripes on walls or use colour to delineate different doors on built-in cupboards. In a shared family bathroom, you need to design a chameleon-like colour scheme. The combination of a sophisticated surface like limestone with a restful palette of taupe, lilac or eau-de-Nil guarantees a bathroom that's grown-up when the kids' things are put away, yet is still an appropriate backdrop for plastic bath toys. Steer kids away from garish novelty character towels, and provide plain ones that complement the rest of the room.

Plan plenty of storage for bathroom paraphernalia, including a high lockable cabinet for any medicines. In a shared family bathroom, give the kids a cupboard for novelty bubble baths and soaps. You won't have to share your grown-up soak with a jumble of bottles, and surfaces are easier to keep clean when free of toiletries. The same principle applies to toys: provide a big plastic bin, and after bathtime they can be tidied away so the space looks sophisticated again. In a kids-only bathroom, display plastic fish and submarines on shelves above the bath.

Play – be it energetic, be it peaceful – is the centralizing force in a child's life, so kids need space to scoot around and spread their toys about. Grown-ups need to be able to tidy it all away. Storage that works is the key.

play spaces

6

THIS PAGE AND OPPOSITE: With forethought, a great play space can be seamlessly integrated into an open-plan living and kitchen area. Modern flooring materials like limestone and concrete are perfect surfaces for toy trains and cars, and, with underfloor heating, are warm and comfortable to play on. If planning a play space from scratch, doors to an outside space are a worthwhile investment. They let in light and increase the play space when open. Fit streamlined and unobtrusive storage. In Pablo's play space, roomy sliding drawers allow him easy access to his toys.

Every child needs space to play. An expanse of floor, a freshly cleared tabletop and enough room to race around are the essentials – without these, children have no free rein with their toys. As adults, we allocate ourselves activity zones: a sofa to sprawl on, a desk for paying bills, an armchair for reading. Children need their own equivalent. It's not fair to tell children they can play all over the house, only to scold them for piling soft toys on the stairs. Try to give your kids a special area where they know they can play. Size isn't the issue – whether it's a patch of floor within a kitchen/dining room, or a separate playroom, what's important is that this is a space they can call their own. Make toys accessible and easy to tidy away, and kids will even enjoy organizing their own private zone.

In recent years, many families have devoted their largest living space to a kitchen, dining and playroom all rolled into one. In a conventional house or flat, an open-plan area is easily created by knocking down walls. But industrial loft conversions are increasingly on the agenda. A decade ago, lofts were the province of the trendy and the child-free. But those same couples are now having families and enjoying the benefits of a vast area of one-level floor space. A loft or warehouse space creates the ultimate indoor playground, with ample room for bike-riding and space-hopping.

The advantages of an open plan living space are manifold. Tiny children can safely play under a grown-up's watchful eye while cooking, watching videos and older kids' homework all get under way. If you're

❝ *This is a really big space for my trains. I like playing here because I'm next to mummy when she's working in the kitchen.* ❞

PABLO, AGE 3 ½

moving house to accommodate a growing family, this is the ideal space configuration to aim for. It's helpful to have a toilet nearby, so little ones don't have to travel too far from their toys. And, if possible, access from the living area/play space to a garden or roof terrace is invaluable. In summer, it doubles the available floor area, while in winter the kids might be more easily tempted outdoors.

If you can't move house, but are adapting your living quarters to accommodate children, think long and hard about the changes you make. You will reap the benefits of employing an architect, although it may seem a major investment at the time. An architect will think more laterally about maximizing space and can squeeze storage into the most unlikely corners. Alternatively, if finances are tight, can rooms be swapped around? Perhaps a dining room off the kitchen could be converted into a playroom, or an underused conservatory adapted into a kids' den? However, if you have a spare room away from the living area that might be converted into a separate playroom, think twice about doing so when your children are small. You won't want to be cooking with half an ear on what's going on next door, and life is infinitely easier if you don't have to call a halt to exciting play in one room and move children to the kitchen to eat. Far better to include the kids' play area within the bosom of the house and get on with the riotous business of family life.

The area chosen for a play space needs to provide a decent amount of floor area for spreading out toys as well as enough room to run around. Make sure everything else going on in the same space won't interfere with the kids' activities, and vice versa. Could you re-route traffic through a play area by moving a sofa to one side of the room? Will you be forever tripping over toddlers while trying to prepare food? If the play space is within or adjacent to the kitchen, safety is vital. Clip trailing wires and cushion sharp corners. Fit cupboards with child locks and plugs with safety covers, and always, always, tuck in saucepan handles.

" It was a way to prevent toys cluttering up the floor. "

FRIEDA, MOTHER

THIS PAGE AND OPPOSITE: While lofts and kids mix well, as there's so much open space it helps adults and children to be tidy if one area is designated as the toy zone. Where there is a very large floor area, building a child-height maze from painted MDF partitions makes good sense, as Juliet and Lucie's parents found out. Make it big enough to hold several little 'rooms' where toy shops or dolls' houses can be permanently located. Painted a strong colour and set amid plain white walls, the maze will become a talking point among adults and a magnet for visiting kids.

The downside of sharing a living space with children is that they bring a sea of brightly coloured plastic with them. It's natural to worry that their arrival may cramp your style-conscious home, yet a minimal interior needn't disappear forever. Rule number one is to provide effective storage so that in the evenings toys can be put away quickly and easily and grown-up order restored. The best solution is to kit out your living/play space with floor-to-ceiling cupboards with flush doors and deep shelves. Locate the kids' things on the lower shelves and use the upper ones for household paraphernalia. If you can, specify extra-deep cupboards so that fold-up dolls' buggies or plastic garages can fit in easily. If there's no room for cupboards, and open shelves are the only option, invest in some decent-looking containers that look good *en masse*. Clear plastic crates and wicker baskets are both practical and stylish.

Rule number two is that precious or beautiful pieces should be put into storage or placed firmly out of reach. If you have the luxury of a grown-ups-only sitting room, then enjoy them in there. It's easy to teach children to respect lovely things and not to draw on the walls, but sensible to accept that accidents will happen. So protect your cherrywood dining table with a wipe-clean PVC cloth and your expensively upholstered sofa with a loose cover in a tough, washable fabric. Replace a limited-edition rug with an abstract one from a chain store. Beaded cushions, velvet throws or anything else labelled 'dry-clean-only' should be removed. Remember, you're creating a child-friendly zone so that everyone can relax.

If you've moved house, decorating and furnishing a play space that doubles as a family living room is great fun. The beauty of integrating kids' stuff with contemporary design is that trendy industrial-style surfaces like stainless steel, plywood and laminate are smart and hard-wearing, and the clear, bright colours of much modern furniture are positively enhanced when littered with toys. When decorating walls, white vinyl matt emulsion creates a simple background, and scuff marks are easily touched up.

ABOVE LEFT: **Every play space needs comfortable, low-level seating for chilling out in front of the video or reading. A simple banquette with comfy cushions, like this one, can incorporate narrow drawers for small toys and jigsaws.**
LEFT: **As an alternative to the ubiquitous miniature table and chairs, a wooden or MDF desktop, fixed on an adjustable rack system, provides a corner for quiet play or drawing and writing, and can grow with the child.**
OPPOSITE: **In a large living room, try to incorporate desk space for older children, for homework, colouring in or for the family computer.**

PREVIOUS PAGES: **With a little judicious selection, there are plenty of playful features that remain easy on the eye once installed in a sophisticated adult space. The key is to use them with confidence, scale them up, and choose colours that will positively enhance the grown-up scheme. Thus, a blackboard can take up half the wall (useful for shopping lists or phone messages), and beanbags can be adult-size and smart with it, perhaps in leather or vinyl. Appropriately placed, a toy such as a bright red child's swing, suspended from the ceiling, can have as much decorative impact as a contemporary chair.**

THIS PAGE AND OPPOSITE: **If space and your budget allow, a child-size heated indoor swimming pool provides kids with the ultimate play space and, if fitted with a swimming current for adults, can be used by the whole family. The parents of these children have positioned a big, comfortable sofa beyond the splashproof glass doors, so an adult can supervise in comfort.**

But have fun with colour too. A single wall painted in vibrant lime green or dazzling bright blue can look stunning, particularly if decorated with children's artwork, properly framed and displayed.

Practical furniture makes life much easier. Polypropylene chairs are a sensible, easy-clean option and 1960s-style versions in vivid tangerine and lime green are great fun. If a table doubles as a dining and painting table, a wipe-clean surface is essential, so a cement or laminated top is ideal. If the table needs to be pushed to one side to create a more flexible space, add castors and the look becomes trendier still. To house the video, choose a long cabinet instead of open shelves. Have a steel one powder-coated in shocking pink, and make a design statement at the same time.

You can be similarly imaginative when selecting fabric for the playroom sofa or chairs. Several bright plains can look stunningly abstract if used as blocks of colour on individual chairs, seats and cushions. Leather is durable and stylish as well as ultra-practical because it is wipe clean. Patterned fabric is excellent for disguising sticky finger marks. Source something bold and wacky that will appeal to both you and the kids: giant cabbage roses on a slim steel-legged sofa, or a 1950s pictorial print of seaside scenes. When it comes to decorating a play space, you can be a little tongue-in-cheek. A 1970s swivel chair upholstered in Mr Men fabric would look suitably funky, as might a giant abstract painting which blurs the barriers between modern art and kids' naïve efforts.

Every play space needs a cosy corner for watching a video or listening to music. If space permits, a small sofa is great for after-lunch naps or quiet reading; if there's no room, beanbags work equally well. Play spaces in communal living areas often have hard floors, perhaps wood or limestone, so a rug or a fluffy faux animal-print throw provides a softer sitting or crawling area for babies and toddlers. Keep the television out of the way by mounting it on a wall bracket or a pull-out arm concealed within a cupboard. But try to site the video at child level, as even two-year-olds will relish the independence of slotting in their favourite film. Provide plenty of storage for videos nearby. They can be fitted into mini plastic crates or stacked in a narrow section of custom-made shelving.

If you're blessed with abundant living space, you can include wacky and imaginative extras. Consider hanging a swing from the ceiling, or keeping a pop-up tent or play house permanently erected. And a child-height mini-maze is not only a wonderful draw for visiting friends, but also an ideal place to keep bigger toys, like fold-out shops and puppet theatres.

OPPOSITE ABOVE LEFT AND RIGHT, AND ABOVE: **Kids glory in the luxury of plenty of play space, yet the adults haven't been forced to compromise their space in these three homes. The modern classic furniture, contemporary sofas in bright colours and casual floor cushions are as trendy as they are child-friendly, so everyone benefits.**
OPPOSITE BELOW LEFT: **A sophisticated adult sitting room can still be family-orientated with sensible choices like washable covers and stain-guarded upholstery. Molly and Eli have soon learned what they can and can't touch.**
OPPOSITE BELOW RIGHT: **When a living room doubles as a play space, there must be plenty of storage for quick tidy-ups. Nica stuffs toys into the retro sideboard and 1970s stacking compartments. Graphic, colourful art will appeal to adults and children alike.**

LEFT: With their vast expanses of floor space, city lofts are wonderful for urban children. There's even room to ride a bike, so on rainy days, kids can get exercise at home rather than struggling to the park. Johanna's parents have a side sitting area where they can relax in comfort while watching the children.

RIGHT: Children relish quirky, one-off pieces of furniture, from outsize lamps to odd-shaped chairs, and will remember such details long after you've discarded them. A long, comfortable sofa, big enough for the whole family, makes an ideal centrepiece, but for practicality stick with strong coloured upholstery or a busy pattern to conceal spills and stains.

spaces to eat

Little ones need a calm and comfortable spot for eating beneath your watchful gaze. Choose wipe-clean furniture and scaled-down shapes, with plates and cutlery in jelly-bean shades, and you'll tempt even the most reluctant eater to the table.

7

Kids' mealtimes may seem like lunchtime at the zoo, but if you choose practical yet good-looking furniture and equipment at least cleaning up will take zero time. In the early years, babies progress rapidly from being spoon-fed to helping themselves in a highchair, then graduating to the grown-ups' table. Whatever stage they're at, the process of getting kids to sit down, eat calmly and observe table manners needs to be achieved with minimum fuss and maximum efficiency. If there is a comfortable eating area, and food is presented attractively, recalcitrant eaters are more likely to hop up to the table.

If possible, situate the table in the kitchen, so you can keep an eye on the kids while preparing food or clearing up. The advantages are obvious – you're on the spot if a child chokes, the kitchen floor is practical and wipe-clean, and food, drink and a damp cloth for sticky faces are all close to hand. Don't despair that your high-tech modern kitchen will be spoiled by highchairs and bright crockery. Source attractive furniture and kitchenware, and the transition will be seamless. Colourful seating, a lime-green toaster or pink plastic beakers will only pep up a stainless-steel kitchen.

THIS PAGE AND OPPOSITE: **These days, it's common for children to gather in the kitchen, so if you're planning a new one make it a stimulating and amusing place to be. This example, with its sweetie-coloured doors and drawers, was deliberately designed with small children in mind. Ease of use is paramount. The long bar handles are simple for kids to grab, and their plates and cups are located in a low cupboard. Island units make sense: children can gather round and help cook, eat meals there, or sit and colour in. Plan plenty of drawers, so that the children's napkins, straws and place mats are easy for them to reach.**

It's fun to provide little ones with a diminutive table and chairs at which they can eat meals or draw and paint. Good-looking styles include miniature versions of the classic Arne Jacobsen 'Ant' chair.

THIS PAGE AND OPPOSITE: It's nice to give children the option of eating at the dining table or at their own special miniature table and chairs set. Choose a big family table, so there's always room for friends, and select a tough tabletop to withstand spills and scratches. Good materials include zinc, stainless steel, cement, marble, slate, laminate or MDF, which can be repainted regularly to cover marks and stains. Save the designer chairs for later years. For a growing family, it's more fun to have mismatched wooden chairs, painted in fun colours, or comfortably upholstered ones with washable covers.

A highchair is essential for babies. Standard designs are practical, but often rather an eyesore. You can either accept this and put up with it, or source a more attractive option. There are simple wooden Scandinavian designs available, or plain white lacquered steel versions. Alternatively, look for a second hand highchair. Repaint it in a bold colour and re-cover the seat in a retro-print oilcloth. You may need to add new safety straps.

If you have older children who eat at the main table, a sturdy canvas or plastic clip-on seat is sociable for older babies, because it fixes onto the tabletop. You might also consider a highchair designed to grow up with the child. These often come in smart chrome and beech. They feature a clip-on tray and safety guard for the baby stage, then adapt, leaving just a useful footrest, into a seat for older children.

THIS PAGE AND OPPOSITE: **It makes sense to think of the children's plates and cutlery as an extension of the adults' options, so the family table looks co-ordinated. Scour the shops for trendy, informal tableware that everyone can share: jewel-coloured tumblers, hand-painted bowls (opposite) and chunky ceramic mugs (below right), ideal for both milk or a cup of coffee. Here, Harry enjoys his cereal from an adult pudding bowl (below centre). Children love pottery-painting cafés, where they can customize their own cups and plates. And buying a picnic set with jolly coloured plates and bowls has a dual function: the kids can use it both on a day-to-day basis and for family outings.**

It's fun to provide little ones with a diminutive table and chairs at which they can eat meals or draw and paint. However, if you like to sit with the kids while they eat, you may not find it such a comfortable option. Eating at a breakfast bar or adding a low countertop to the end of an island unit might be a more casual, user-friendly solution. The choice of small scale tables and chairs has increased recently; look in high-street stores, kids' catalogues or grown-up contemporary design emporia. It's also worth investigating nursery furniture designed for schools. Good-looking styles include miniature versions of the classic Arne Jacobsen 'Ant' chair, chunky wooden seats in primary colours or whitewashed Swedish-style tables and benches. You can match the style to your kitchen.

The sooner you encourage small children to sit up at the grown-ups' table, the better; it socializes them, and fosters a sense of independence. If you have a beautiful table, protect it with a PVC cloth at all times. The same

ABOVE: **Retro highchairs are by far the most tasteful versions on offer, so scour junk shops for old wooden models that can be enlivened with glossy paint or fitted with a new laminate tray. Choose a style that harmonizes with the other chairs around the table, so that baby can join in stylishly at mealtimes!**

goes for upholstered dining chairs: it may sound like an investment to have a set of loose covers made up, but the upholstery will be saved from sticky fingers. If you are choosing new chairs for family mealtimes, look for polypropylene, metal or wood. Light chairs in plastic or aluminium are good, because a small child can manoeuvre one by himself. Pick a style that is comfortable for kids as well as looking smart. A slatted seat can trap fingers, while a chair with arms won't pull close enough to the table for a small person to eat in comfort. School-style benches are also excellent, providing plenty of extra room for friends. High stools at a breakfast bar are great for older children, but be sure little ones won't overbalance.

With imaginative shopping, you and the kids will find laying the table positively creative. Tiny versions of anything will delight them, and a choice of colours is great, because each can pick their favourite shade. Not everything has to be plastic, although picnic sets in dayglo colours are a good source of plates

and cups. Duralex glass tumblers are virtually indestructible and come in appealingly small sizes. Many casual dining ranges are in robust pottery, and traditional enamel plates and cups are also hard-wearing. These days, many manufacturers produce bright-handled cutlery in small sizes. Customize place mats: draw on slate slabs with chalks or transfer a favourite photograph onto mats at a specialist store. Alternatively, scour design shops for wacky wipe-clean place mats and pictorial napkins.

Everything to do with kids' mealtimes should be accessible for them, as it encourages setting the table from an early age. Store bowls and cutlery in a low cupboard and drawer and keep lunchboxes in there too. Is the fridge easy for an older child to open, so they can help themselves to snacks? Is there a sturdy stool for a little one to hop onto so he can get a drink of water from the tap? The easier you make eating and drinking for your children, the sooner they will be integrated into the sociable world of family mealtimes.

ABOVE: **Miniature table and chair sets needn't be clumsy pieces of moulded plastic in garish colours. For an individual and stylish look, choose more elegant versions that mimic grown-up contemporary classic styles, such as these little moulded beech veneer 1960s-style chairs (above left).**

spaces for storage

Call it paraphernalia, equipment, toys or simply stuff, children have an alarming number of possessions. If the whole family is to enjoy a peaceful and efficient living space, then it's up to you to squeeze great storage out of every square centimetre.

8

New parents soon learn that children come complete with lots of stuff. Over the years, regular clear-outs will help, but the fact remains that the minute you start a family your need for hard-working storage increases tenfold. After the baby bouncer and sit-on fire engine come fleets of tiny cars and dolls' accessories, then home-made models, musical instruments, tennis rackets, and more. Accept the influx with good grace, and set about planning where everything should go. It's a cliché, but a place for everything is the ultimate aim, even if frenetic family life doesn't allow for an 'everything in its place' conclusion.

However capacious the storage in the kids' bedrooms and play space, there will be yet more stuff you need to house in heavy traffic areas like the hall. Ask yourself where outdoor gear – coats, hats, kiddie umbrellas, boots and buggies – will go. What about sports equipment – ballet and swimming bags, footballs and cricket bats? The older children get, the bigger the kit becomes. Bikes need a home, as do tents, sleeping bags and outdoor games.

If there is room in your hall, a run of cupboards will hold all the essentials and keep things tidy. Consider wall-mounting them, leaving room beneath for shoe storage. For small children, a low row of pegs on the wall is better: outdoor gear can be seen at a glance and little ones may be more inclined to hang up their bags. Use a big basket or galvanized metal tub to hold shoes, and another for hats, scarves and gloves. A low bench where children can perch while doing up their shoes should be situated near the coat rack. Pick one with a lift-up lid and extra storage within. If bikes are a problem and the hall is high enough, fit them onto a wall rack. Alternatively, store them in the garden or build a lock-up store at the front of the house.

In the long, narrow halls typical of nineteenth-century houses, there's space for little more than peg rails and an umbrella stand. Storage must be squeezed in elsewhere – perhaps in an understairs cupboard, or incorporated into shelves or cupboards in the play area. Don't expect everyday gear to be stored in the children's bedrooms:

LEFT: **When a bedroom is also a playroom, cupboard doors that conceal toys will guarantee more restful bedtimes. Style needn't be sacrificed to practicality: plan cupboards as part of an overall decorative theme. In this loft, plexiglass and plywood cupboards are used throughout, not just in the child's room; translucent materials are a good choice if a wall of doors threatens to overpower a room.**
RIGHT: **Capacious toy drawers hold lots and are easy for children to reach. Be imaginative with the drawer fronts: cut out patterns from MDF fronts or choose stainless-steel or painted wood fascias.**

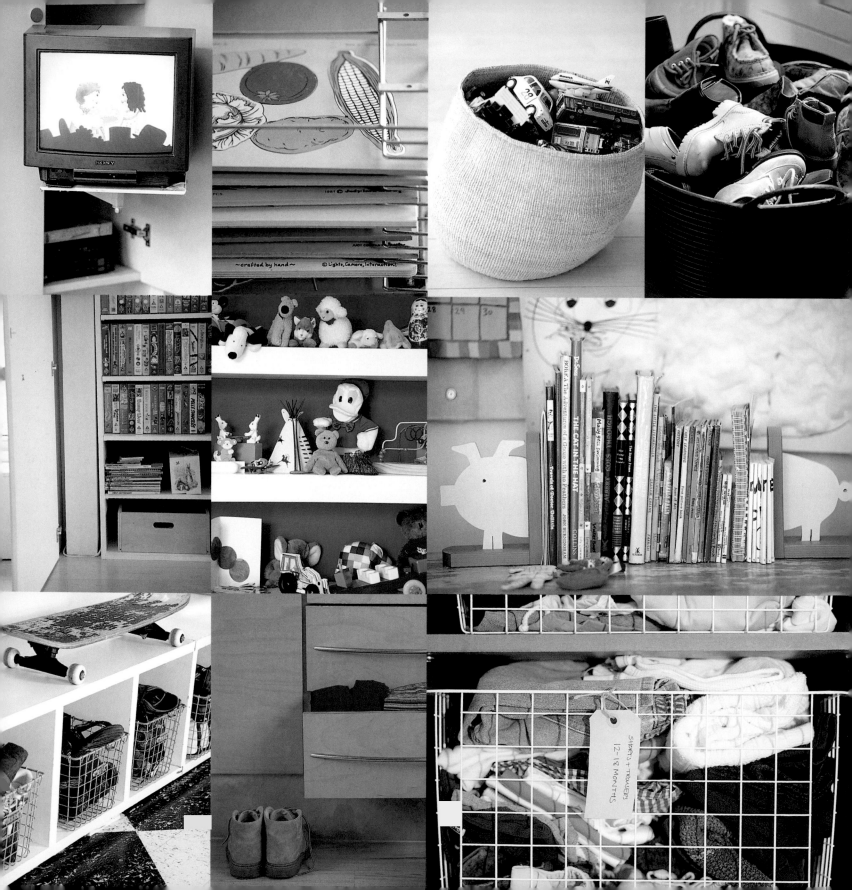

PREVIOUS PAGE: **Of course, large cupboards and deep shelves are essential for storing toys, but just as crucial is the need for plenty of individual containers. Give children the means with which to compartmentalize their toys and involve them in the process of organization, so there are individual homes for pens, plastic animals, building blocks, books, toy cars and so on. Anything can be pressed into service as a container, from galvanized metal buckets to sisal baskets. See-at-a-glance storage is the most helpful, so choose open-topped wicker baskets, transparent plastic crates or screw-topped glass jars – boxes with lids are harder to tidy quickly. Label everything, so both kids and adults know what lives where.**

ABOVE RIGHT: **If you're planning a family home from scratch, a separate corridor running along the side of the house can be devoted to bikes, outdoor gear and sports equipment. Here, wall-mounted cupboards create a spacious effect and there's a stone floor, so muddy boots and wet coats can be removed before children enter the house.**

OPPOSITE: **Even in a small hall, provide a child-sized stool or bench so kids can sit down and pull their boots and shoes on and off. If there's a place for everything – designated coat pegs, an umbrella stand, bike racks and hooks for school bags – your family will have no excuse for mess!**

you need everything to hand for the early-morning rush. However, an array of hanging bags and coats will look messy in an open-plan living and play area. A smart solution is to build a grid system of shelves, each just big enough to hold a labelled wicker basket, and pack everything in. Perhaps a cupboard in the utility room could hold outdoor gear, while open shelves by the back door are good for shoe storage.

In the kitchen/living/play space, it's essential that you and the kids have enough storage for day-to-day paraphernalia so everyone stays organized. Display the school calendar, reading lists and sports fixtures on a giant pinboard, and if its messy appearance spoils a smart dining area, hang it on the inside of a cupboard door. If the play zone is part of the kitchen, clear a kitchen cupboard or drawer so that hairgrips and brushes, museum pamphlets, painting equipment and Play-Doh are easily tidied away, yet can be found when needed. If you are planning a kitchen from scratch, consider a central island unit with drawers and cupboards that can be devoted to your children's clutter.

T-SHIRTS

VESTS

SOCKS

THIS PAGE AND OPPOSITE: Tailor-made storage may seem like an indulgence, but it makes daily activities like nappy changing and getting the kids dressed much simpler. Lots of little compartments are the key to good organization. List the things to be stored, from cotton-wool balls to baby vests, then provide equally well-regimented cubbyholes. Stack see-at-a-glance glass-fronted cabinets with open-topped storage boxes, line a shelf with wicker baskets, or make a decorative feature out of labelling individual drawers. Customize wherever possible: if a cupboard lacks sufficient compartments, then add your own MDF divisions.

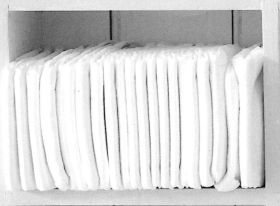

Built-in storage needs to look fabulous as well as being practical – so design it as an integral part of your decorating scheme, not as an afterthought. If you have one baby now, double the storage you've planned because it will all be used eventually. For the smartest, neatest look, fit doors on all your shelves. They can be wide and sliding or narrow and flush, with finishes in everything from painted MDF to sand-blasted glass, zinc, Perspex or wood. Avoid open shelves: lovely as they look when just built, the clean, clutter-free look will be gone once they are crammed with toys, books and equipment. Use every spare centimetre of space. Floor-level drawers are great for toys, while a narrow alcove can hold bookshelves. There's still a place for freestanding furniture, but go for quirky pieces that add character, like an old metal sports locker.

There's no point having good storage if children won't use it. Make it so simple for them that there can be no arguments. Handles should be easy to grip, so look for metal D-handles, recessed door pulls and chunky knobs. Keep some shelves shallow, so items don't get lost at the back. Within a cupboard, divide up paper, pens, scissors and glues within small plastic crates, sisal baskets or good old-fashioned baked-bean cans. Compartmentalize drawers with shop-bought dividers or make your own from sections of MDF. And label boxes and crates. If the children can't read yet, use a Polaroid picture of each toy type for reference, or colour-coding: red for books, blue for cars and so on. When an activity is finished, teach them to put everything away before they start the next game. It's a lesson we adults could do well to learn, too!

Kids love outdoor spaces, where they can run, jump and play crazy games. Give them a secret hideaway and they'll disappear for hours. It doesn't matter whether you have a modest city garden or huge lawns — any outdoor space allows children to let off steam.

outdoor spaces

9

Let children loose in an open space and they're off, tearing about with all the delight of a puppy off the leash. If properly wrapped up, they rarely notice if it's cold and the grass is wet, and on a summer's day will happily stay outdoors till dusk. Try to give them some outside space. We can't all have vast lawns, but even a tiny backyard or roof terrace has potential for creative play.

Design's current obsession with the indoor–outdoor principle has many benefits for children, and is the perfect solution in a small urban patch. A play space that opens straight onto the garden makes outdoors very accessible. Children can run in and out and are easily visible to adults within. If your property doesn't allow for this arrangement, consider the exit points from the house. Ideally, kids should be able to get in and out by themselves, so French or sliding doors are ideal. If the only access to the outside is through a 'precious' adult sitting room with a carpeted floor, could you create a new door, perhaps via a utility room or the kitchen?

THIS PAGE AND OPPOSITE: A conservatory playroom gives the best of both worlds: in Lucy and Sisi's, the door can be thrown open on sunny days, and they get the benefit of lots of daylight, even in winter. Blinds are a must, to guard against glare and keep the room cool. Consider running the same flooring from inside to outside – concrete, stone or hardwood – for practical and aesthetic reasons. A conservatory playroom needs robust, weatherproof furniture, so that it isn't a disaster if a chair is left outside overnight, and should also provide sufficient storage for larger outdoor play equipment.

THIS PAGE AND OPPOSITE:
Nothing beats the appeal of an outdoor playhouse, however rudimentary. It's relatively simple to adapt a shop-bought DIY wooden shed, customizing it with a 'gingerbread' roof trim or a stable-style door. Ensure the playhouse is waterproof, then help your children decorate the inside, perhaps with a painted wooden floor or even wallpaper. For proper imaginative play, the house must have a window and a door. Fit in chairs and a table, for impromptu meals, and supply big galvanized metal bins or wicker baskets for chucking toys into at the end of the day.

The whole point about children playing outside is that they should be able to do so unaccompanied – it's no fun playing cowboys and Indians with a grown-up standing by. Tiny ones do need more of a watchful eye. Before you let them loose, make sure children will be absolutely safe. Fit the back gate with a lock and check they can't climb over the fence or fall over the edge of a roof terrace. Are all swings, ropes and treehouse ladders secure and well-supported? Water features, from a tiny pond to a swimming pool, must be made child-safe too. Somehow, you need to make the kids feel free, while still keeping a close watch on what they're up to. One option is to create a screen separating a children's play area at the bottom of the garden from the rest of the lawn. Construct it from large-scale trellis or bamboo, so you can see through the gaps. And a treehouse should be visible from at least one window in the house.

A playhouse is always a winner. Children love the idea of a private space of their own, and they can store all their outside toys there. There's no need to spoil your garden with a garish plastic structure: the wooden variety is much more tasteful. However, custom-made children's cottages can be ruinously expensive. Far better to design your own and get a carpenter to make it, or even to adapt an ordinary garden shed. So long as the structure has a door and windows, it will be heaven for little girls and boys. Reach a stylistic compromise on the decoration. If you choose to paint the exterior in a subtle colour like lichen green, allow the kids to design the inside. Staple-gun fabric remnants to the inside of windows for curtains, and add little chairs and tables. If budget permits, a more sophisticated summer house can be fitted with water, electricity and heating. It could even double up as a home office or guest room.

A treehouse or raised platform between branches will double the appeal of being outdoors. You could make it to scaled down proportions, so that only kids can squeeze through the opening into the 'house'. Or build it big enough for the whole family to enjoy an evening meal up there. Apart from ladders, all sorts of extras can be added. Suspend a hammock, hang a string of Chinese lanterns, a rope ladder, climbing rope or a swing. While a treehouse blends best into the tree if built from hardwood, you could paint it a bright colour and turn it into the central focus of the garden.

When planning child-friendly outdoor space, divide up the available space into specific activity areas, using a scale plan if necessary. Ideally, there should be a running-about area, a deck designated for a table and chairs, and a secret play area, perhaps with a sandpit, usually at the end

THIS PAGE AND OPPOSITE: By incorporating a few imaginative features into your garden, you will fire your children's imagination. A densely planted area, with a mirror on one wall, becomes a fairy grotto at the bottom of the garden, while a *trompe-l'oeil* gate suggests a secret world beyond. Break up a boring expanse of lawn with pretty picket fencing or fast-growing plants like bamboo, so there are secret spots for a private picnic or games of hide-and-seek. Always secure any exits from the garden so everyone is safe. Provide children with fun equipment so that playing outdoors becomes an extension of inside. Here, Yasmin and Sarah let off steam with a giant ball.

of the garden. If you have older boys, you might instead want to allocate the bottom of the garden for football. Keep their scuffed piece of lawn out of sight by disguising it with a dividing section of wall or fence. In a bold modern garden, the wall could be turned into an architectural feature and painted in a vibrant hue. Alternatively, integrate it into the rest of the garden by growing a flowering creeper over it, and fit with a pretty wall-mounted fountain. Think about imaginative ways to mark out the different activity areas. You could use tall plants, stepping stones set into the lawn or trellis. And, although vast, manicured lawns are great for running round, and an ideal spot for the trampoline or climbing frame, kids do

PREVIOUS PAGE: **A great child-friendly garden has a structure to climb on, be it a simple rope swing or full-blown treehouse, a quiet area for drawing or eating and a stretch of grass to run around on. Relaxed planting means kids don't have to steer clear of special flowers; or teach them to respect the garden by giving them their own patch. Plan sunny and shady areas. If there's no natural shade, provide a sun umbrella or little tent, or grow a creeper over an arch.**
THIS PAGE AND OPPOSITE: **Well supervised, kids will spend hours playing in water. Provide inflatable boats and animals, plus flippers and snorkels, and blow-up rings for younger ones. For Bo, Tucker, Gibson and Gussie, the pool is the place to be.**

appreciate a touch of nature's chaos. Section off a part of the garden, plant it with bamboo, palms, wild grasses and flowers, and you won't see your kids for dust.

If your outdoor plot is very small, such divisions are impossible, so concentrate instead on making the space attractive for grown-ups yet user-friendly for kids. Laying the same flooring throughout instantly unifies a tiny garden: limestone, wooden decking, quarry tiles and cement are all good options. Don't sacrifice running-about space by having large flowerbeds: stick to robust, evergreen shrubs in tubs, which not only look stylish but will also withstand the odd knock from a football. Hard surfaces are practical, but children also appreciate a spot of grass where they can flop down and read. A circle of turf, however small, can look very chic surrounded by limestone flagstones, and allows sufficient space to pitch a tiny tent.

Provide access to sand and water in the garden, and you'll keep younger children amused for hours. Shop-bought sandpits often come in garish colours, so consider building your own. If creating a small city garden from scratch, a sandpit can be inset into the hard floor, but fit a tight cover so that sand is protected at night. An outdoor tap, easy enough for a child to turn on, means little ones can fill buckets or water the garden to their hearts' content. It's relatively easy to plumb in a hot-water tap too. Add a giant planter beneath it, and the children can indulge in a marvellous hot bath in the open air. With safety in mind, a fish pond is best saved until the teenage years. But it's still possible to enjoy water features: choose a wall-mounted fountain with self-circulating pump, so that

" Friends come over and the children can do their thing – having a pool is the greatest form of entertainment. " DEB, MOTHER

the water goes round and round, instead of pooling into a potentially fatal trough.

Eating outdoors is exciting for children and fun for adults too. Choose all-weather metal or wooden furniture that can be left out the year round, so that impromptu alfresco meals are easy. Look for miniature versions of teak garden furniture or tiny deckchairs in bright canvas. Building a wooden arbour for trailing flowering plants or a vine provides essential shade. And a family barbecue, beneath its leafy cover, is the stuff childhood memories are made of.

THIS PAGE AND OPPOSITE: **Instead of fretting about the limitations of a small, urban outdoor space, concentrate instead on finding fun ways to equip it for play. With a water pipe, paddling pool and hose, this small rooftop eyrie is an irresistible draw for three-year-old Teresa on a hot day. Water play equipment is inexpensive and fun: look out for giant water pistols, or spray and jet attachments for a conventional garden sprinkler. Pick a rigid rather than blow-up style of paddling pool, as it will double as a sandpit. When space is short, fold-up mini-deckchairs, pop-up tents and blow-up armchairs are all good choices.**

stockists and suppliers

BED LINEN

Laura Ashley
Call 0870 5622 116 or visit
www.lauraashley.com for details of
your nearest store or for a home
furnishings catalogue.
Co-ordinating fabrics, bed linen
and ready-made curtains featuring
flowers and maritime motifs.

Couverture
310 Kings Road
London SW3 5UH
020 7795 1200
www.couverture.co.uk
Kids' hand-embroidered bed linen
and cotton pajamas, plus soft toys,
baby quilts and retro china.

Damask
3–4 Broxholme House
New Kings Road
London SW6 4AA
020 7731 3553
www.damask.co.uk
Cot and bed quilts in pretty
florals or appliquéd space and
fairy designs.

Designers Guild
267–271 Kings Road
London SW3 5EN
020 7243 7300
www.designersguild.com
Bright animal- and flower-print
bed linen with co-ordinating
fabrics and accessories.

Mothercare
Call 01923 210 210 or visit
www.mothercare.com for details of
your nearest store.
Colourful cellular and fleece baby
blankets, co-ordinating bedding
ranges and nursery furniture.

FURNITURE

Back in Action
11 Whitcomb Street
London WC2H 7HA
020 7930 8309
www.backinaction.co.uk
Children's chairs and tables, plus
furniture to help good posture.

The Conran Shop
81 Fulham Road
London SW3 6RD
020 7589 7401
www.conran.co.uk
Simple, contemporary cherrywood
beds, changing units and chests of
drawers, plus polypropylene tables
and chairs and fun accessories.

Habitat
Call 0845 6010 740 or visit
www.habitat.net for store details.
Metal bunk beds, colourful
melamine desks and wardrobes,
beanbags and miniature table and
chair sets.

Heal's
Call 020 7636 1666 or visit
www.heals.co.uk for store details.
Contemporary children's furniture
and accessories, including wooden
bunk beds with storage beneath.

Noel Hennessy Furniture
6 Cavendish Square
London W1G 0PD
020 7323 3360
www.noelhennessy.com
Quirky flower-, heart- and cloud-
shaped tables and chairs in
primary colours.

IKEA
Call 020 8208 5600 or visit
www.ikea.com for details of your
nearest store.
Inexpensive, flat-packed modern
bunk beds, desks, storage units,
miniature tables and chairs, plus
lots of fun accessories.

Next Home
Call 0845 600 7000 or visit
www.next.co.uk for details of your
nearest store.
Metal bunk beds and bright
beanbags, plus funky bed linen,
shower curtains and storage items.

Oreka Kids
020 8884 3435
www.orekakids.com
Manufacturers and suppliers of
Biscuit plywood kids' furniture,
including fun folding tables, a
storage bench and a wardrobe.

Lena Proudlock
01666 890 230
Ready-to-paint wooden children's
tables, chairs and benches in
simple Swedish style. Also
colourful denim beanbags.

Purves & Purves
80–81 Tottenham Court Road
London W1P 9HD
020 7580 8223
www.purves.co.uk
Bunk-bed systems with clip-on
accessories plus unusual wooden
toys and kids' lighting.

Stokke UK
Call 01895 442 990 or visit
www.stokke.com for details of your
nearest stockist.
Manufacturers and importers of the
Scandinavian Tripp Trapp chair,
which grows up with the child.

MAIL-ORDER CATALOGUES

The Great Little Trading Company
08702 414 080
www.gltc.co.uk
Outdoor play equipment, mini-
deckchairs, storage ideas and great
gadgets, plus personalizing service.

Alice Hart & Company
PO Box 176
Beckenham
Kent BR3 6ZG
020 8663 1248
www.alicehart.co.uk
Pashmina and fleece blankets,
simple wooden furniture, pyjamas
and christening gifts.

L & T Morgan
01227 713 973
Simple painted furniture, including
a snakes-and-ladders table and
Noah's Ark toy box, plus a Shaker
four-poster child's bed.

Urchin

Call 01672 872 872 or visit www.urchin.co.uk for stockists. Practical and contemporary furniture, accessories and gadgets for trendy babies and kids, from mobiles to beanbags and fun tableware.

The White Company

Call 0870 160 1610 or visit www.thewhiteco.com for stockists. Bed and cot sets in embroidered white cotton, gingham sheets and pure wool blankets. Also Moses baskets, bath towels, towelling robes, pyjamas and slippers.

BEDS

Bed Bazaar

The Old Station
Station Road
Framlingham
Suffolk IP13 9EE
01728 723 756
Specialists in reconditioned antique beds, including school and hospital bedsteads, also mattresses in unusual and small sizes.

Bump

020 7249 7000
www.bumpstuff.com
Ready-to-paint MDF sleigh beds, bunk beds and daybeds.

Harriet Ann Beds

Cherry Garden Farm
Hastings Road
Rolvenden, Cranbrook
Kent TN17 4PL
01580 243 005
Great selection of antique wooden sleigh beds. Mattresses and small sizes available, or original designs made to order in reclaimed pine.

The Iron Bed Company

Call 01243 578 855 or visit www.ironbed.com for details of your nearest store. Iron bedsteads, also available in small sizes, hand-painted with a soldier or sunflower design.

STORAGE

The Holding Company

241–245 Kings Road
London SW3 5EL
020 7610 9160
www.theholdingcompany.co.uk
Ingenious sisal baskets, plastic and canvas boxes, drawstring bags and hanging racks. Catalogue available.

Muji

Call 020 7323 2208 or visit www.muji.co.uk for details of your nearest store.
Huge selection of steel shelving as well as cardboard, acrylic, fabric and polypropylene storage boxes.

FABRICS/WALLPAPERS

Cath Kidston

51 Marylebone High Street
London W1U 5HN
020 7935 6555
www.cathkidston.co.uk
Simple florals in pretty colours, with matching oilcloths, retro children's fabric cushions and a bathroom-motif wallpaper.

John Lewis

Oxford Street
London W1A 1EX
020 7629 7711
www.johnlewis.com
A good source of inexpensive ginghams and plain cottons, plus patterned PVCs for tablecloths.

The Natural Fabric Company

Wessex Place
127 High Street
Hungerford
Berkshire RG17 0DL
01488 684 002
www.naturalfabriccompany.com
Basic fabrics, with plain cottons, checks, ginghams and denims.

Nobilis-Fontan

Chelsea Harbour Design Centre
London SW10 0XE
020 7351 7878
Whimsical, abstract French children's fabrics and wallpapers, including a design with fish in trees and a fairy on a bike.

BATHROOMS

First Floor

174 Wandsworth Bridge Road
London SW6 2UQ
020 7736 1123
Stockists of Dalsouple rubber floor tiles, lino and vinyl tiles.

C P Hart

Newnham Terrace
Hercules Road
London SE1 7DR
020 7902 1000
www.cphart.co.uk
Wide range of contemporary wall-hung sinks and baths in every size.

Pipe Dreams

72 Gloucester Road
London SW7 4QJ
020 7225 3978
www.pipedreams.co.uk
Scaled-down toilets and basins in any finish, including glittery pastels.

ACCESSORIES

Brats

281 Kings Road
London SW3 5EW
020 7351 7674
Eclectic selection of fake grass tiles, kitsch accessories and Miffy items.

T A Cartlidge

020 8265 0444
Hand-crafted dolls, made to commission.

The Cross

141 Portland Road
London W11 4LR
020 7727 6760
www.thecrosscatalogue.com
Trendy accessories, including pretty Chinese lanterns, soaps and monogrammed cushions.

Mathmos

20 Old Street
London EC1V 9AP
020 7549 2700
www.mathmos.co.uk
Contemporary lighting, including the original lava lamp in many colours.

The Rug Company

Call 020 7229 5148 or visit www.rugcompany.co.uk for stockists. Contemporary and traditional floor coverings.

Urban Outfitters

36–38 Kensington High Street
London W8 4PF
020 7761 1001
Kitsch accessories, including funky shower curtains and sparkly lamps.

10

picture credits

All photographs by Debi Treloar unless otherwise stated.

Key: l left r right b below t top c centre

2 An apartment in London by Malin Iovino Design; 3 Vincent & Frieda Plasschaert's house in Brugge, Belgium; 5 The Boyes' home in London designed by Circus Architects; 12–13 Victoria Andreae's house in London; 14–15 Ab Rogers & Sophie Braimbridge's House, London, designed by Richard Rogers for his mother. Furniture design by KRD–Kitchen Rogers Design; 16–17 Sophie Eadie's house in London; 18–19 Rudi, Melissa & Archie Thackry's house in London; 20 tl & br An apartment in London by Malin Iovino Design; 20 bl Designed by Sage Wimer Coombe Architects, New York; 21 Vincent & Frieda Plasschaert's house in Brugge, Belgium; 24–25 Julia & David O'Driscoll's house in London; 26–27 Ben Johns & Deb Waterman Johns' house in Georgetown; 28–29 Michele Johnson's house in London designed by Nico Rensch Architeam; 30–31 The Zwirner's loft in New York; 34–35 Designed by Sage Wimer Coombe Architects, New York; 36–37 The Boyes' home in London designed by Circus Architects; 38 Designed by Sage Wimer Coombe Architects, New York; 42–47 Victoria Andreae's house in London; 48–49 Sera Hersham-Loftus' house in London; 50 l Suzanne & Christopher Sharp's house in London; 50 r–51 The Zwirner's loft in New York; 53–55 Sudi Pigott's house in London; 56 Elizabeth Alford & Michael Young's loft in New York; 57 Sophie Eadie's house in London; 58–59 Julia & David O'Driscoll's house in London; 62–65 Eben & Nica Cooper's bedroom, the Cooper family playroom; 67 Sue & Lars-Christian Brask's house in London designed by Susie Atkinson Design; 68–69 Pear Tree Cottage, Somerset, mural by Bruce Munro; 70–71 Suzanne & Christopher Sharp's house in London; 72 & 73 br An apartment in New York designed by Steven Learner Studio; 73 tl & tr Vincent & Frieda Plasschaert's house in Brugge, Belgium; 74–75 Ben Johns & Deb Waterman Johns' house in Georgetown; 78–79 Vincent & Frieda Plasschaert's house in Brugge, Belgium; 80 bl Sophie Eadie's house in London; 80 bc David & Macarena Wheldon's house in London designed by Fiona McLean; 80 br Sera Hersham-Loftus' house in London; 81 bl & br Ben Johns & Deb Waterman Johns' house in Georgetown; 84 l Ab Rogers & Sophie Braimbridge's House, London, designed by Richard Rogers for his mother. Furniture design by KRD–Kitchen Rogers Design; 84 br Designed by Ash Sakula Architects; 85 An apartment in New York designed by Steven Learner Studio; 86 Sudi Pigott's house in London; 87 Ben Johns & Deb Waterman Johns' house in Georgetown; 88–89 photographer Caroline Arber/Archie & Pink, London E1, loft designed by Will White; 90–91 David & Macerena Wheldon's house in London designed by Fiona McLean; 92–93 Vincent & Frieda Plasschaert's house in Brugge, Belgium; 94 tl Designed by Ash Sakula Architects; 94 b An apartment in London by Malin Iovino Design; 95 Ben Johns & Deb Waterman Johns' house in Georgetown; 96 main An apartment in London by Malin Iovino Design; 96 tcr, lc & lb Belén Moneo & Jeff Brock's apartment in New York designed by Moneo Brock Studio; 96 tr Ben Johns & Deb Waterman Johns' house in Georgetown; 97 main Elizabeth Alford & Michael Young's loft in New York; 97 tl & tr An apartment in London by Malin Iovino Design; 98–99 Hans & Lena Blomberg's house designed by Orefelt Associates; 100 tl An apartment in London by Malin Iovino Design; 100 tr Vincent & Frieda Plasschaert's house in Brugge, Belgium; 100 bl An apartment in New York designed by Steven Learner Studio; 100 br Eben & Nica Cooper's bedroom, the Cooper family playroom; 101 tl Ab Rogers & Sophie Braimbridge's House, London, designed by Richard Rogers for his mother. Furniture design by KRD–Kitchen Rogers Design; 102–103 The Zwirner's loft in New York; 106–107 Designed by Ash Sakula Architects; 108 l Victoria Andreae's house in London; 108 r Sophie Eadie's house in London; 109 l David & Macarena Wheldon's house in London designed by Fiona McLean; 109 r The Zwirner's loft in New York; 112 l Victoria Andreae's house in London; 112 r The Zwirner's loft in New York; 113 l & r Designed by Sage Wimer Coombe Architects, New York; 116 & 117 tr Belén Moneo & Jeff Brock's apartment in New York designed by Moneo Brock Studio; 117 bl & bl Designed by Ash Sakula; 120 David & Macarena Wheldon's house in London designed by Fiona McLean ; 121 Designed by Sage Wimer Coombe Architects, New York; 122 tr & b & 123 Victoria Andreae's house in London; 126–127 Michele Johnson's house in London designed by Nico Rensch Architeam; 128 l Ben Johns & Deb Waterman Johns' house in Georgetown; 128 r Victoria Andreae's house in London; 129 Charlotte Crosland's house in London; 130–131 playhouse by Dan Levy; 133 main & tc, cr, & br Sarah Gredley's house in London, tree house designed by Kim Woolfe-Murray; 134–135 Ben Johns & Deb Waterman Johns' house in Georgetown.

architects & designers credits

Elizabeth Alford Design
60 Thomas Street
New York
NY 10013
USA
t. 001 212 385 2185
f. 001 212 385 2186
e. esa799@banet.net
56; 97 main

Ash Sakula Architects
38 Mount Pleasant
London WC1X OAN
t. 020 7837 9735
www.ashsak.demon.co.uk
84 br; 94 tl; 106–107;
117 bl & br

Circus Architects
1a Summer's Street
London EC1R 5BD
t. 020 7833 1999
f. 020 7833 1888
5; 36–37

Charlotte Crosland
Wingrave Crosland Interiors
t. 020 8960 9442
f. 020 8960 9714
129

Malin Iovino Design
t. 020 7252 3542
f. 020 7252 3542
e. iovino@btinternet.com
2; 20 tl & br; 94 b; 96 main;
97 tl & tr; 100 tl

KRD–Kitchen Rogers Design
t. 020 8944 7088
e. ab@krd.demon.co.uk
14–15; 84 l; 101 tl

Dan Levy
artist / woodworker
34 Summerfield Ave
London NW6 6JY
t. 020 8969 8428
130–131

Fiona McLean
McLean Quinlan Architects
t. 020 8767 1633
80 bc; 90–91; 109 l; 120

Jeff Brock and Belén Moneo
Moneo Brock Studio
371 Broadway, 2nd floor
New York
NY 10013
USA
t. 001 212 625 0308
f. 001 212 625 0309
96 tcr, lc & lb; 116 & 117 tr

Bruce Munro
Mural commissions
t. 01749 813 898
f. 01749 813 515
e. brucemunro@freenet.co.uk
68–69

Nico Rensch Architeam
t. 0411 412 898
28–29; 126–127

Orefelt Associates
4 Portobello Studios
5 Haydens Place
London W11 1LY
t. 020 7243 3181
t. 020 7792 1126
e. orefelt@msn.com
98–99

Sage Wimer Coombe Architects
480 Canal Street
New York
NY 10013
USA
t. 001 212 226 9600
f. 001 212 226 8456
20 bl; 34–35; 38; 113 l & r;
121

Susie Atkinson Design
t. 0468 814 134
67

Steven Learner Studio
307 Seventh Avenue
New York
NY 10001
USA
t. 001 212 741 8583
f. 001 212 741 2180
www.stevenlearnerstudio.com
72; 73 br; 85; 100 bl

Kim Woolfe-Murray
Urban & Country Tree Houses
34 North Junction Road
Edinburgh
EH6 6HP
t. 0131 553 5554
133 main, tc, cr & br

Will White Design
326 Portobello Road
London W10 5RU
t. 020 8964 8052
f. 020 8964 8050
e. willwhite.design@virgin.net
88–89

index

acknowledgments

Thank you to Anne Ryland, whose eyes lit up, instead of glazed over, when I first mooted the idea
of a *children's* contemporary decorating book.

A huge thank you to Debi Treloar, for her limitless energy, amazing patience with children and
fabulous photographs. To Louise Leffler, for her deft creative vision; to Kate Brunt, for tremendous
locations; and to Gabriella Le Grazie, for her watchful eye. Thank you Alison Starling and
Annabel Morgan, for your spot-on editorial support.

Thank you to all the parents, who so kindly welcomed us into their private family spaces,
and to every child we photographed. It was a privilege to see your bedrooms,
guys – I hope we didn't tidy up too much!

Thank you Anthony, Cicely and Felix. Our family life has been the inspiration for this book. And thank
you to *my* parents, Harry and Ann, who when I was a child generously humoured my nascent decorating
streak and let me design my bedroom at a very tender age.